How Do I Write My Life Story?

Helen McKenna

ISBN-13: 978-0-9924363-4-6

Website: www.helenmckenna.com.au

Published by Lightning Source

CONTENTS

"Life is what happens when you're busy making other plans…"

(John Lennon)

I WANT TO WRITE MY LIFE STORY

Writing about your life is a wonderful thing to do. Unfortunately, many people don't do it because it seems very difficult to accomplish and/or they don't know where to get help and advice on how to go about it. This book is aimed at the average person who has the desire to record their life story but isn't sure where to start.

In my experience, the majority of people wanting to write their life story are of retirement age, so this book is targeted largely at that audience. However, the technical information on how to get your story written is relevant across all age groups. (If you are younger you can ignore some of the generational references and no doubt you will already be confident with technology). The overall process is still the same no matter how old you are.

The first thing to remember is that **anybody** can write their life story. You don't have to be famous or even well known. Most people who write their story won't go on to have it published and made into a best seller. But that doesn't matter. Many people just want to write things down for their family and friends – so others can understand a bit more clearly what their life has been about. It's also a wonderful legacy for future generations of your family to treasure.

You may feel that you haven't made any great impact on the world – you haven't travelled far and wide or made any great scientific discoveries. However you have no doubt accomplished far more than you realise in your everyday life and these seemingly average life events are what children and grandchildren love to hear about. If you've even had an inkling that you might like to record your life story, then have a go at doing it. The information on these pages is there to help and encourage you.

If you are reading this book, I presume that you don't have a lot of writing experience. That is not a problem – that is why this book exists. Like any talent, there are some people who are better at writing than others. But that doesn't mean that those with less experience can't build up their skills and make a good job of recording their life story.

Some of you may follow this book from beginning to end, take on board all the advice and complete the extra exercises at the end. Others may only undertake certain parts. That, of course is totally up to you. Try to be open-minded though. At least read the whole thing through from start to finish and then decide which path you're going to take.

There are, of course, ways that you can enhance your writing skills before you start your story. One of those is to join a writer's group. Don't get put off by the name. You don't have to be a published author to be in a writer's group – in fact you don't have to have written anything. All you need is an interest in writing and a willingness to participate. (See page 94 for further details about writer's groups).

Another way is to undertake a short writing course either by correspondence or at an adult education centre, TAFE college or other training college or university (see page 101 for further details). There are specific courses that deal with writing your life story.

A third way is to read books about writing. Check your local library or bookstore – there are many titles out there aimed at helping the novice who wants to improve their writing skills.

Something else that may help you prepare for writing your life story is developing (or brushing up on) your computer skills. Don't freak out – I'm not saying you have to – but if you have any interest in learning how to use a computer, it will make writing your life story much easier. Not just because you can type it up on the computer yourself, but also because you can use the internet to research and seek out information along the way (especially when you get to the editing stage). For those of you who are already computer literate, those skills will be very helpful in the weeks and months to come. If you can use a computer but don't actually own one yourself, now could be a good time to get one.

There are lots of computer courses out there – either at TAFE or other adult education centres or through senior citizens/community centres. Perhaps you could get a family member or friend to show you the ropes. If you can already type, you are well and truly on your way to being able to use a word processing program. Having said that though – you do not need any computer skills to physically write your story and I'm not pushing you in that direction if you don't want to go there.

Don't be surprised if you get some discouragement along the way. You may be told it's too difficult for a non-professional to write a decent life story or that the writing process will stir up old emotions and painful memories. The first point is simply not true. Yes, it may be *more* difficult for a non-professional to write a life story but nothing in life is *too* difficult if you put your mind to it and have a plan in place.

As for stirring up old memories, well yes, no doubt you will experience some emotional upheaval – but does that have to be a bad thing? Prepare yourself for it and then work through it. Most people who write their story find it a cathartic experience and a way to cleanse themselves of old demons that still haunt them. Remember, too that you are in control of what you write about. If you believe something will be too difficult to cope with then don't include it in your story at all.

You have probably picked up this book because you have been considering the idea of writing your life story (either recently or for several years). Maybe you have a child or grandchild who wants you to do it. Whatever your reasons, if you've come this far, make a commitment to having a go. By reading this book and following the advice contained within it, you WILL be able to come up with your own story.
I am not promising that you will be able to whip up a cracking good yarn headed straight for the best-seller list, but I am saying that you can

produce something. Whether it be a very basic, no-frills chronology of your life or a colourful, entertaining story – you have taken the step of getting it down on paper. If you struggle to go beyond the bare facts, you can get some help further down the track to turn it into something more. If you are ready to really embrace the elements of writing, the tools you need are within these pages.

Although not essential, it is very beneficial to build yourself a good support network before you start. Unless you are an extremely private person or are completing your story as a surprise, let your family and friends know what you are doing so they can support you along the way. Whether it be your spouse or children giving you the space to write in peace, old friends helping you reminisce or getting together a group of like-minded people to write your stories together – let others help you where they can. If you aren't computer literate, you will need some assistance along the way – so start thinking about who you can ask.

All right, let's stop procrastinating and get started. I suggest you read the book right through and then go back and work through each section. Progress at your own pace, but make a firm commitment to set aside some time each week and you will get there.

Finally, GOOD LUCK! You CAN do this.

GETTING STARTED

When writing the story of
your life, don't let anybody
else hold the pen.

Rebel Thriver

STARTING OUT

The thought of writing your life story can be daunting! It *is* a big undertaking and it *will* take time and effort to see it though. However, it is also a very rewarding thing to do and the personal fulfilment of completing your story is well worth the time and effort required. The key is to tackle it bit by bit.

Like any big project, you should have a plan in place before you begin. Having a plan will make the writing of your story official and really bring the idea to life. It will also make the task seem much more manageable.

Writing your life story is not one of those projects that you can 'knock together' over a couple of weeks. Nor is it something you should rush through as fast as possible. To do the best possible job you need to allow yourself time for preparation, research, writing and then editing (with breaks in between so you don't burn out). That's not to say that you can't get it done reasonably quickly if you're motivated, but be realistic in your expectations. Six months is probably the minimum you should plan for.

Remember writing is a creative process, which can sometimes be frustrating. Any writer (even an accomplished one) will agree there are times when you just can't come up with a single sentence. They key is not to let that frustration put you off. Set your story aside for a few days or a week and then come back to it with renewed enthusiasm and try again. Don't ever give up!

Finally, you don't need any special equipment to get your story down on paper. Using a computer will make the job easier, but it is not necessary – writing can still be done the old-fashioned way! I have edited many wonderful stories that were presented to me in longhand. So don't use that as an excuse any longer.

CREATE YOUR PLAN

To start with, think about the autobiographies or memoirs you have read. Which one(s) did you like best? Were there any you identified with? Was there a particular style you would like to emulate or a certain theme you would like to base your story on? If you haven't read very many biographies/autobiographies go to a library or bookshop and look at some. Read, or at least flick through a couple. It might not be the whole book, but just different aspects of it that you like. Note down any ideas as you go. For example, do you like a 'warts and all' approach, where any topic is open for discussion or would you prefer to be more selective in what you include? (There is a comprehensive list of titles at the end of this book if you need some inspiration. Or you can simply find the autobiography/biography section at the library or bookshop and browse the titles there).

Next, decide what form your story is going to take. Just to be clear there is a difference between an autobiography and a memoir. An autobiography is the story of your entire life, generally from your earliest memory until the time of writing. A memoir, on the other hand, focuses on only one (or sometimes a few) areas of your life – for example your childhood, war experiences, career or sporting achievements. It is more like a collection of stories rather than a chronological account of your life.

How are you going to physically write it – longhand? Or on a typewriter or computer? Typewritten work is neater but some people prefer to handwrite, which is fine. Some like to handwrite first and then type it up later. Another option is to use a tape recorder (refer to page 48 which deals with oral recording).

Note down your ideas about what to put on the cover. Most people choose a photograph of themselves (either a current one or a favourite childhood one), but this is not mandatory. For example, you could use a family photograph (like Hugh Lunn on *Over The Top With Jim*), a picture of your childhood house or a favourite place. The possibilities are endless.

The title of your story is another important detail. Some people are happy to simply call it 'My Life' or 'My Story' while others like to be a little more creative. If you don't have a definite idea, list a few possibilities to mull over. (Refer to page 89 for an exercise to help you select a title.) On the other hand, don't spend hours agonising over it if you don't have an idea to begin with – put it to the back of your mind and come back to it later.

Consider the approximate length and whether or not to include photographs and other mementoes. If so, list which photos and mementoes.

Finally give yourself a rough time frame to complete the project. This doesn't have to be set in stone, but like any deadline it will keep you motivated. As I mentioned before, be realistic. Allow for the day to day activities you still have to undertake, a possible illness (eg cold or flu) and seasonal events like Christmas, Easter, birthdays and other family events. Remember you can always revise your plan later if you know you won't get it done in the time allocated.

While creating your plan is important, don't worry if you don't come up with *all* the answers concerning finer details right off the bat - you have plenty of time to think about them as you go along. Also, you are not locked into any of these decisions. You are free to change your mind and have different ideas along the way.

MAKING NOTES

Now you have a plan in place, it's time to start making notes. I know there are some people reading this book who don't think they need to do that. They've already got some good ideas in their head and just want to get on with it. While it may seem like an unnecessary step, making notes is actually very important. It is the framework on which your story will be built. If you take the time to make thorough notes, you will have a strong base which you can draw on as you write your story. If you decide to skip this step, your foundation will be weak and any time gained by racing ahead will be lost as you flounder and struggle to keep on track.

Some people have amazing memories and can remember past events with crystal clarity in great detail. Don't worry if you can't do that - there are many ways you can unlock hidden memories from your subconscious. The following pages contain many triggers which will soon have your transported back in time.

No matter how good or bad your memory is; the foundation of your life story should be a 'memory notebook', where you can record brief notes that you can refer back to later. We all know how things can slip in and out of our minds very quickly, so it is important to get into the habit of writing information down as you remember it.

I use the term notebook loosely - it can be an exercise book, A4 paper, the back of used envelopes – whatever you want to use to write things down. If you are using loose pieces of paper, make sure to keep them all together (eg in a folder or cardboard wallet).

If you find you are remembering things at random times (eg when you're shopping or on the bus/train), try and keep a smaller notebook and pen with you that you can combine with your main notebook later. If you are tech savvy, use your smartphone or iPad/tablet.

1, 2, 3......GO!

Start your note taking off with a 'brainstorming' session. Take a large piece of paper (butcher paper is ideal) and make yourself comfortable. Then, off the top of your head, jot down in point form the things in your life you could possibly write about. It doesn't matter how roughly you do this – just note whatever comes to mind. If you want to enhance your creativity use coloured pens or textas. Have fun with it and include everything, no matter how insignificant it seems. You can weed out the unnecessary stuff later.

You will probably be amazed at what you come up with in this very first activity, even if you don't consider yourself to have a particularly good memory. Spend at least an hour on brainstorming – more if you want to.

After your initial session, put the piece of paper aside, but keep it handy. (If you can, leave it somewhere that you don't have to pack it up each time you use it). Over the next few weeks, continue to record things as you remember them. Now that you have started to stir up old memories, you will find things start popping into your head all the time. Write them down as you think of them!

SOME IDEAS TO GET YOU STARTED

Check the following list for ideas. You can do this either before or after you initial brainstorming session. It is not an exhaustive list – there are hundreds of other things that could be included.

Your immediate family – parents, siblings, grandparents, cousins, aunts/uncles. Were your parents strict? Were you a close family? Did you get along well with your brothers and sisters? Did you see your relatives often? Did you have a favourite/least favourite relative?

Your house – What kind of house did you have (eg Queenslander, Terrace)? How big was it? Was it neat and orderly or messy and 'lived in'? How many bedrooms? Did it have an indoor or outdoor bathroom? What was the backyard like? Where did you play? Did you have any privacy?

Your town/city - Where? Was it a large city or a small town? What was it like during your childhood compared to now? Where did children go to play or meet friends? Did you roam all over the place or were you strictly supervised? Were the streets reasonably safe for children to play in?

Your school – Was it a neighbourhood public school or a private school? Was it strict? Did you ever get the strap or the cane? Did you have to wear a uniform and/or shoes? How did you get to school? If you walked how far was it and how long did it take you? Did you have many friends and who were they? Who were the good and bad kids in your class? Did you have a favourite teacher or one that you really didn't like? Did you do well at school and did you enjoy it? How long did you stay at school and what exams did you pass? What was the leaving age in your time?

Leisure time – did you get much time to yourself while growing up? What games did you play as a child and who with? Did you have any special hobbies or interests? Did you take part in any extra activities like music lessons, tennis or ballet?

Birthdays/Christmas – how were these celebrated in your family? What was the build up like? Did you ever long for a particular present? What kind of food did you eat on these occasions?

Family activities – did you have particular activities that were an integral part of your early life – for example going for family drives or walks or picnics? What about family holidays – where did you go and how regularly? Did you have a set routine at home – was a roast lunch on Sunday as certain as the sun coming up?

Music – did your family have a radio (or wireless)? What kind of music did you like to listen to? Did you have any favourite groups? Did you have a record player?

Religion – Was your family religious? Did you go to Church every Sunday or to Sunday School? Did religion influence your family life a lot? Did you have to say your prayers every night? Did your religious beliefs influence the decisions you made?

Food – What were mealtimes like in your house? Did you sit together for your evening meal? What kind of food did you eat? Did you have set meals for each night of the week? What did you consider to be a real treat? Did your mother do all the cooking and baking or were you expected to help out too? What kind of stove did you have? Did you have a refrigerator?

Chores – were you expected to do a lot of chores around the house? Did they take up a lot of your time? Did you enjoy any of them or did you find them all to be the bane of your life? Did you ever dare to complain that you didn't want to do your chores?

Adventures – did you have any adventures that you still remember fondly now? Did you ever go off exploring with a group of kids just for fun or sneak into a place that you weren't allowed to go? Did you ever find yourself in danger?

Dreams/ambitions – did you have any special dream(s) or wishes as a child or teenager that you were determined to fulfil? Did you spend hours daydreaming about it? Did you tell anybody of your dream or was it something you kept private? Did you ever realise your dream(s) as you got older? If not do you regret not pursuing it more fully? Is it something you could still achieve now?

Finances – were your parents well off or were they battlers? Did they manage well on a tight budget or did you have to go without a lot of things? Did you grow your own food or keep animals to keep costs down? Did a lack of money ever concern you or did you think it was the norm because all your friends were the same?

Friends – what kind of friends did you have? Were you one of the popular kids or more 'middle of the road'? What kind of things did you and your friends do? Have you maintained any friendships throughout your life that were made at a very young age?

Pets/Animals – did your family have any pets? Were you an animal loving family? If you did have pets where did you get them from – was it a pet shop or were they strays? Were you and your siblings expected to look after them?

Your first job - What was it? Was it full or part time? How old were you? What was your hourly or weekly pay rate? Was your wage yours to keep or did you have to contribute to the family income? Did you have to attend an interview or do an exam or were you just told when you could start? Did you enjoy your work?

Career - What jobs have you done since that first one? Did you have to study or do training for in your particular field or was it on the job training? Did your parents/teachers influence the career you chose or was it your own decision? Did you feel restricted by the choices that were available to you? Have you enjoyed your work or do you wish you had done something else? Any highlights?

Your spouse(s) – when and where did you meet each other? How long did you go out for before you were married? What kind of places did you go to on dates? What kind of wedding did you have – was it a lavish affair or something small and simple?

Your children and grandchildren – how many children/grandchildren do you have? Were they energetic and mischievous or quiet and well behaved? What were some of the things they did that almost gave you a heart attack? Did they suffer from any illnesses or injuries and did this affect the family in any way? What have they done in their lives?

Parental Influence – Do you think that your parents have influenced your life in many ways? Did you continue to ask their advice even when you had your own family? Have the values they taught you reflected in your own family life? Have you remained close to your siblings and other extended family as you have gotten older?

Travel – have you travelled very much? What places have you been to and at what age? What would you consider to be your favourite place/s? What have you gained/learned from travel? Do you consider holidays and travel to be a priority in your life or only something that can be done when you have time and money? Have you become a 'Grey Nomad' or are you planning to?

Your house/houses – how many different houses/flats have you lived in since leaving home? Did you build, buy or rent them? How many different towns have you lived in? Which place(s) did you like best?

Your Hobbies/Interests/Passion - have you continued with your own personal interests and hobbies throughout your adult life? Is there something you love to do and spend all your spare time doing? Or is there something you would *like* to spend time doing but you just never seem to get around to it?

Lessons learned - what would you consider some of the true-life lessons you have learned and who/what taught them to you? Is there anything about your life you would change if you could?

Remember at the note-taking stage you don't have to record things in great detail. You're not writing the actual story yet. Just jot down enough to remind you what the particular memory is. A couple of sentences are usually enough.

On the other hand, there's no point writing down one or two words if it's going to take you hours to remember what you were thinking of. If you don't have a great memory, write more rather than less.

Even at this stage, take care to keep your work legible and number your pages to keep them in some kind of order. Keep all your notes together. As previously mentioned a folder or cardboard wallet is ideal.

A Few More Memory Triggers

Visit or phone people that you have known for a long time and have a reminiscing session. Isn't it true that such conversations can bring back many memories – things that you hadn't thought about for years? Make notes or record your conversation to keep a record.

If you or any of your friends/family have **diaries,** then read them and make notes - or get the other party to read them (if they are private) and pass on any pertinent information. Diaries are a wonderful memory aid because the information is there in a person's own words and in many cases, it can be very detailed. Diaries can often contain some hidden surprises or remind you of things that you had long forgotten.

Do a **time breakdown** of your life – for example you might choose five-year blocks. For each of these blocks write down the major events that happened during this period of your life. Some of these things might seem too obvious or trivial to make a note of (eg 'bought a new car'), but they will help you to build a bigger picture of that period of your life. To use the car example - how did your new car affect your life? Did you work hard to afford it or did you have to go into debt? Was that good or bad? Did it give you independence and freedom that you never had before?

Use major **historical events** as a memory aid. We all have a list of these in our minds. For example can you remember when the Queen came to visit? Where were you, and what were you doing when you heard about JFK being shot? Do you remember the start or end of World War II? The day man walked on the moon? If you can't remember the exact date of the historical event in question then look it up so you are sure about the time period you are writing about.

Letters and cards you have kept throughout your life can contain a huge amount of information. Even a basic appointment diary can contain a surprising amount of detail. Perhaps a particular business deal or meeting was a very important turning point in your life.

Watch movies or mini-series that are set in a time period that you have lived through and pay special attention to such things as clothes, cars, public transport and houses. Observe social customs – for example how men and women greet each other, how different classes interact and the different words and expressions people use. Look out for particular products like washing powder or cosmetics. Some examples of mini-series that could be useful are: *Harp In the South/Poor Man's Orange* (1950s), *Brides of Christ* (1960s), *Vietnam* (1960/70s), *The Shiralee* (1940s), *A Town Like Alice* (1940s), *The Dish* (1960s), *Bodyline* (1930s), *All the Rivers Run* (1900s).

Read books (both fiction and non-fiction) that are set in a particular era. Can you relate to the characters and the experiences they had? Were there any similarities in your own life? Pay attention to the kind of language used. So many words have disappeared from the Australian vocabulary over the past fifty years it is easy to forget such words and the associations they may have held for you at a particular time. You could even make a separate list of these 'forgotten' words and use them as a reference point to help to really capture a particular time period.

Check if your local library has old newspapers on microfiche or in an digital format (most do). Set aside a few hours and look through old papers. As well as the actual news stories look at the advertisements (what products and what prices) and photographs of the area (especially if it is an area that has changed and grown a lot). See if you remember any of the stories and consider if they are worth including in your own story, if it had some impact on your own life. Look at the wedding and engagement notices and pictures. If possible, check the day you were born and see what else was happening in the world on that momentous day.

Listen to old music from whatever time periods you are reminiscing about. Music can evoke many powerful memories.

Look through your old photos. To get the maximum amount of information from each photograph ask yourself such questions as:

- How when and where was the photo taken? Is there a date and/or names written on the back?
- Was it for a special event or occasion? If so what was it?
- What clothes are you wearing? Were they special clothes, school clothes etc?
- What can you remember about the actual day that the photo was taken?
- Was it taken at your home or somebody else's?
- What can you remember about the house? What was the furniture like? Did you have a special place that you used to play?
- Was it taken at a special place outdoors like on a picnic or a holiday?
- Are there other people in the photo? If so what are five things that you can remember about each person?
- Are there any animals or pets in the photo? If so what can you remember about them?
- Can you remember who took the photo and whose camera they used?

Two Little Assignments

Allow yourself at least a month to make your notes (more if you think you need it). Even if you get to the end of two weeks and are SURE there is nothing else you can remember, don't rush ahead. Instead, before you start writing, you should undertake these two assignments.

(1) Read and study at least five autobiographies (this can include titles you have already read). If you want to do more than five, go ahead – in fact the more you read the better. You don't have to wait until you have finished your notes to start, you can be reading while you work on them. You can even start reading the autobiographies before you begin your notes if you like.

When I say study these books, I mean pay attention to the format of the story, the kind of language used, how the author may have interwoven historical events into their story, how many photographs they have included, if there is a strong theme, the titles of the books (and how the title relates to the story), how many chapters and how long each chapter is, what is on the cover, what is on the blurb on the back and so on. You aren't studying other people's work with the intention of copying it. The purpose of this exercise is to get you very familiar with an autobiography, so you know what you are aiming to create for yourself.

Check the list on page 83 for some ideas or go to the library and have a look – there are hundreds out there. Obviously you should choose ones that interest you – this is supposed to be an enjoyable assignment.

Two things in particular you should look at are the beginning and end of each story. There are many different ways you can start and finish an autobiography or memoir and it is very helpful to get some ideas circulating in your mind before tackling your own masterpiece.

(2) Writing your life story is a great reason to get all your old photos sorted and put in order. Ask around your family members and friends and find out who has old photos and exactly what they have. Then decide which photos you would like a copy of and either find somebody within your family/friends who have the equipment to scan and make copies (chances are there will be) or find a professional to do it for you. Any photo shop such as Camera House will probably have a photo restoration service or will be able to recommend one. Most Kmart/Big W/Harvey Norman stores do photo processing. There are also small operators around who specialise in restoring and digitalising old photographs and slides. Generally, the more you get done the cheaper it is.

It is amazing what can be done with old, torn, creased and small photos. Black and white images come up particularly well. It doesn't matter if colour prints have faded or discoloured (early colour film didn't have the longevity of modern film) – this can also be corrected (or the photo can be altered to black and white or sepia).

You don't need negatives (although they are useful if you have them) and once you have a digital file (the same as the file created using a digital camera – JPEG for example) you can distribute them to anybody who wants them. You can also get as many reprints made as you want at little cost. (All camera shops as well as Kmart/Big W/Harvey Norman have processing centres for digital photos. The cost per print is much less than having a reprint made from a negative. If you're not confident using the self-serve equipment have a family member or friend help you or ask for assistance from a staff member).

Of course, if you have a lot of old photos yourself, this can also be an opportunity to distribute them to other family members/friends as well. You don't have to have dozens of prints made; you can just have them compiled on a CD, which can then be easily distributed. Once you've got your photos in order, redo the memory exercise listed on page 23 for any new photos you now have.

MORE WORDS TO TRIGGER MEMORIES:

washing day

school milk

backyard dunny

the ice man

clothes props

the wireless

slates at school

getting the cuts

scholarship exam

white cotton sheets

bluebag on bee stings

wearing a hat to church

braces on men's trousers

bowler hats

corsets

castor oil

hats and gloves

Catholics vs State School kids

unsupervised play until dark

bread and dripping

no seat belts

wooden tennis rackets

white sandshoes

unwrapped white bread

sleeping on the veranda

manual telephone exchanges

hitching rails for horses

six o'clock pub closing

oil spraying at the beach

chip heaters

unlocked houses

hand-me-downs

flypaper

nurse's veils

milk in glass bottles

records and record players

milkshakes in steel cans

trams in Brisbane and Sydney

sing-a-longs around the piano

nibs and inkwells

slingshots

home-made bloomers

cooking in lard

nuns and brothers

home movies with no sound

black and white photos

chicken on special occasions only

mosquito nets

going to school barefoot

having only one set of good clothes

drink driving was socially acceptable

air raid shelters

patients rolling bandages in hospital

heating the iron on the stove

Saturday mail delivery

kids having their own air rifle

Girl Guides and Boy Scouts

canvas tents with no groundsheet

slingshots

whole family sharing the bath water

driveway service at petrol stations

Saturday afternoon at the pictures

groceries being home delivered

un-chlorinated swimming baths

fish and chips in newspaper

white walled tyres

news reels at the movies

polishing your shoes

ORGANISING

At this stage, you might be feeling a little overwhelmed! You probably have pages and pages of notes, but they may seem disjointed and disorganised. Or some of them might overlap and you feel like you've repeated yourself. Don't despair - instead take some time to sort your notes out before you begin writing the actual story.

Your main aim at the organising stage is to break your story into sections. Take some blank pieces of paper (or a new section in your notebook) and write some headings – for example: early childhood, parents, siblings, primary school, high school, first job, travel etc. Or you could do three or five-year blocks or whatever else makes sense to you. Chronological order is probably the easiest.

Now go through your notes and transfer all the points/notes you've made into their appropriate sections. Make sure you leave some space at the end of each section to add in any extra memories you may come up with. Keep your work well spaced so you can see at a glance what is in each section. As you work through your notes cross off each thing as you transfer it, just to keep track.

Your notebook/folder doesn't have to be immaculately neat and in precise order - just make it an easy reference point for yourself by arranging it in a way that you will be able to access and follow easily. If using loose paper, a folder is a great idea to keep everything together. If you are computer literate using a word processing program like Word is ideal to get your notes in order.

Once you have all your points/notes in their correct sections, take some time to do your first cull of unnecessary information.

Firstly, check for anything that you have listed twice – maybe use a highlighter or a red pen to show what needs to be removed.

Then have a closer look at what else you have put down. While it might be interesting trivia about your life and a particular era in general, you aren't going to be able to use all of it in your story. For example, if you lived on a farm and had a large array of pets, listing them all by name and giving a full physical description of each won't be very exciting to most of your readers. Nor would a complete explanation of each house renovation you undertook or sewing project you created. That's not to say you can't use the information in a general way – ie. you can mention that you renovated eleven houses, but just don't go into detail about each one (unless it is particularly relevant to the story).

If you have points that overlap, take a closer look and see how you can merge different things together. Sometimes you can use poetic licence to combine several similar events, rather than mentioning each single one. As long as it's not something that is a crucial event in your life, some of the smaller details don't need to be one hundred percent accurate.

Similarly to de-cluttering your home, it gets easier to weed out unnecessary information the more times you do it. On your first cull it can be hard to let go of various facts that you have worked long and hard to remember, but you will become more ruthless as you progress through your story. If in doubt leave it in for the moment, you can come back to it later and make a decision then.

CHECKLIST FOR PART ONE

Before moving onto the actual writing of your story, make sure you have your basics covered.

★ Firstly, is it going to be an autobiography or memoir? Choose one or the other and go with it – don't chop and change or you will drive yourself crazy.

★ Is there anything that needs extra research? This can be family information or local/national/worldwide events. Make sure you have your facts correct – not just the way you remember something happening. That's not to say you can't bring your own recollection into it – but you need to know what you're comparing it to. Talk to family members to get family stuff right (or check genealogical records if you have them) and use the library (either encyclopaedias, the internet or newspapers on microfiche) for historical specifics. If you don't have the basic facts right your story loses credibility.

★ Think some more about your title. If you haven't come up with a definite title yet, list at least five possibilities and/or try the exercise on page 97.

★ If you are going to handwrite, your work will need to be typed up at some point. Will you be able to do it yourself or will you need to get someone else to do it? Who could you ask – a family member or friend? Or are you prepared to pay someone to do it for you? Get this organised now so you aren't delayed further down the track. Maybe you could ask a few different people to spread the load a bit.

Writing The Story

There is no greater agony
than bearing an untold
story inside of you.

Maya Angelou

WRITING

At this point it's important to come up with a routine that will allow you to be as productive as possible. Look at your plan and see how long you have allotted yourself to write your story, then break that timeframe down into weeks/months and work out the minimum time you'll need to commit each week to meet your deadline. Accept that you may need to adjust your timeframe as you go.

Try to set aside a particular time, or times, each week (or day) to work on your story and don't allow yourself to be distracted. This may mean shutting yourself into a different room, going to the library or sitting outside somewhere. If you tend to get a lot of phone calls consider putting the answering machine on, taking the phone off the hook or putting your mobile on silent while you work. If you are using a computer, turn off your internet connection when you are writing (unless you are specifically researching something). It is VERY easy to get caught up in mindless web surfing and lose hours of productive time. If you can manage to write every day (even if just a paragraph or two) you will build up a great momentum. Many professional authors maintain that is the rule they work by.

Choose a time when you work most effectively. For some people this is early morning, for others late at night. You might be somewhere in between. Also work with your own concentration span. Are you a person who does things in short bursts or can you sit down and work for a reasonably long time? Don't set an impossible goal of four hours if you know you will be distracted after forty-five minutes. Have all the things you are likely to need close by so you don't have to keep getting up. Keep your notes in order. Choose somewhere comfortable where you can spread out as much as you need to. Preferably make it somewhere you don't have to pack up each time you finish. Every writer needs their own little haven to be as creative as possible.

SOME WRITING TIPS

First and foremost, if you are handwriting, you need to keep it legible. There is nothing worse than going back to read something later and not being able to understand what you've written. It also makes it easier if you want somebody else to read it. Keep your writing well-spaced and leave a generous margin on both sides.

Feel free to use your own words and expressions in your story. It is about you and should reflect your personality. Obviously, you should keep it to things your readers will understand, but don't think that you have to write in the Queen's English or to use complex words or phrases. In fact, you should do the opposite. Simple, informal language is much more appealing to a reader.

Don't be *too* concerned about spelling and grammar as you go along. They can (and should) be corrected later. If your spelling and grammar is not the best, worrying about getting it right can really slow you down. It's better to get the gist of your story down (with errors) rather than laboriously written pages that take forever to complete. Remember you should enjoy the process as much as possible.

Tackle one section at a time. It's easy to get flustered if you don't give your full attention to what you've chosen to work on today or this week. Remember you don't necessarily have to start at the beginning. If the thought of writing about your early days is a bit daunting, start with something more recent. Once you get into the flow of writing you will build up momentum to go back and tackle the more challenging parts.

Don't panic if you realise you've left something out or you think of another event or detail after you've finished a particular section. It is very easy to go back and change things – there is no limit on the number of drafts you can do. Write down what you want to include and just make a note of where it slots in with the rest of the story. If you're using a computer, you can amend it on the spot.

It doesn't matter if particular sections have more detail than others. Inevitably there are parts of your life that you remember better or that were more important to you. It makes sense to write about them in more detail. If you decide that a particular section could do with some more detail, then use some of the memory trigger techniques to help flesh it out more.

Remember that you are writing about things as you saw them. Don't be scared to include something that other family members or friends may disagree with. As the author of your story you are entitled to write things according to your own recollections. Different slants on the same event can all be true and that is what makes autobiographies so interesting. Like a reporter documenting a news event through their eyes, you can similarly document the events that have made up your life.

On the other hand, don't fictionalise things to settle an old score against somebody, to seek revenge or to just stir up trouble. With the benefit of hindsight and the wisdom of years we can all see things differently. So you might describe an event and explain how you felt *at that time* and the effect it had on you. Then you could explain how you *currently see* the same event. This doesn't mean that the event didn't have an impact or that you weren't wronged, it just means that you can see it for what it was at the time it happened.

If you can't decide whether to include something or leave it out, include it for the time being. Reading over it yourself or having others read it will give you a better indication of whether it's appropriate to leave it in. Think very carefully before including something just for 'shock' value. While it may add drama and perhaps intrigue to your story, remember this is also a legacy to your family members and once something is written and 'out there' it can't be un-said. Don't let one event overshadow the rest of your story. Sometimes discretion is the best way.

Ultimately, you have to be the judge of what kind of language you use and how much you want to say about more personal issues. You might not find swearing particularly offensive, but some of the people reading your book might. Consider who will read it and what age they will be. Think about what you would like people to get out of your story. Then do what you think is appropriate. You could even have a "test" reader give an opinion before making a final decision.

BUT HOW DO I START?

Most people would argue that you should start writing your story at the beginning and work through it chronologically, but as mentioned before, you don't have to. You could pick a point anywhere in your life and start with that and go back and do the beginning later. Do whatever feels right for you.

Before you start writing think back to the autobiographies you have just read and how each author started their story. Some simply start 'I was born on….. in the town/city of….' and there is nothing wrong with that – but there are more creative ways to begin and no doubt you have read a few of them.

Some set the scene using a historical moment: …. "World War Two was in full swing when I came into the world on June 5th, 1940. Although my father was too old to serve (at the ripe old age of thirty-six) three of my uncles were in the Middle East and my grandmother was heavily involved in the war effort…"
OR you could mention the seasons or something relating to your family circumstances… 'It was the coldest winter in a decade when I arrived on the world scene on July 15th, 1957. Frost was thick on the ground and Dad had to spend ten minutes de-icing the windscreen of his ancient truck, before he could respond to my mother's increasingly desperate pleas to get her to hospital….'

"… as the seventh child in my family (and four years after my next-in-age sister) I'm not sure if my birth was greeted with as much joy as my eldest brother's, but my mother always assured me I was a welcome addition to our family, even if I was a 'surprise'….."

Even if you don't know of something specific about your birth date, try and relate it to something else either by researching (old newspapers as previously mentioned), speaking to a family member or friend who might remember or just use the facts you have to put a different spin on the plain facts of your birth.

Some people begin their story with a prologue or preface, which is an introduction before the main story begins. Generally, authors who do this pick a fairly recent moment in their life and then 'flash back' to their birth and the story of their life. Dawn Fraser, for example, used the moment she was crowned *World Swimmer of the Century*. A prologue or preface is usually fairly short, generally a few pages.

Another option is to use the introductory paragraph(s) as a mini prologue. Sara Henderson starts with the moment she was awarded Businesswoman of the Year. Janine Shepherd's story begins when she wakes in hospital after her horrific bike accident.

Still unsure about where to start? Have a look at a few more autobiographies. Go to the library and study the beginning paragraphs or pages of another four or five of them, and see if anything strikes a chord. If you are still struggling to come up with your introduction, don't get stressed out about it. Get something down on paper – whether it be a simple few sentences….I was born on…etc – or whatever you can come up with – and get on with the story. Leave it at least a few days and then come back and have another try, then another if necessary. Don't waste days or weeks trying to come up with the perfect introduction on your first attempt – leave it as a work in progress. You might not come up with something you're happy with until you've finished your first draft, which is totally fine.

Getting those first few sentences down can be difficult. However, once you've got that out of the way, you will really feel like you've begun. Always try and sit down to write in a positive frame of mind and believe that you CAN produce something worthwhile. Not everybody is a born writer, but like many skills you will get better as you go along. In fact the more you write, the more momentum you will build.

WORKING THROUGH THE STORY

I am a big believer in the first draft being a bit of a dumping ground for ideas and thoughts without trying to get it perfect on the first attempt. You may think it seems like a waste of time to have to go back and change things later, but in writing you need to move through several stages before a polished story emerges at the end. Even if you are a perfectionist, accept that your first draft is not your final version.

When I say a dumping ground, I don't mean to churn out pages of mindless drivel – just don't deliberate over every word before you put it down – otherwise your story will never get written. If you're caught up in telling an exciting event, just write it as it comes to mind (sometimes your hands won't be able to keep up with your brain – either on a keyboard or with a pen) and don't worry too much about getting it technically right. If you're writing about something that needs a lot of description, include everything that comes to mind to begin with. You can scale it back later.

Try to create rough paragraphs as you go, so your writing is not one continuous block of text. Don't worry too much about the technicalities of paragraph creation (we will get to that in the editing section), but each page should have at least three or four paragraphs if possible. If you have some writing experience and want to create your chapters as you write, then go for it – but if you're a novice, just leave it for now. We will get to that later.

SCENE BY SCENE

A story is not just a collection of words, sentences and paragraphs – it is a compilation of scenes, each of which builds on the one that came before it. In basic language a scene is a piece of a story. Each scene generally happens in one place at one time and, thus, when you change the scene, the time and place also changes. A change of scene is generally indicated by a line space, or it can be a whole new chapter.

The thought of writing your story can be much less daunting if you think of it on a scene-by-scene basis, rather than as a whole. For example, if you say you are writing a 40 000-word story, that seems like a massive undertaking, but if you refer to it as 100 scenes, each 400 words long – it seems more achievable. It is one of the ways you can keep yourself from getting overwhelmed.

Like your entire story, each scene within it should have a beginning, middle and end. No reader likes to be dropped in the middle of a new scene without being guided there. It's confusing and annoying. To begin your new scene, you should be clear about where you are (both physically and geographically) and if a period of time has elapsed since your last scene. You don't have to document things down to the day/hour – but give a general idea so your readers don't get lost as to where you are and what you're doing. If something dramatic is going to happen build up to the action slowly, don't hit your reader over the head with it before they're made aware of what's going on. The beginning of the scene is when you do this.

The middle of your scene is the action part. Each scene needs to have a point to it and the middle is where the story plays out. What happened - and more importantly - how did it happen? If there is no clear point to your scene you should remove it. However, if there is information in the deleted scene that you believe to be important to the story, work out another place that information can be slotted in without having to be a scene on its own. Often things can be spoken about (ie dialogue between characters) or it could be something your own character thinks about.

The end of your scene wraps things up. It shows the outcome of the event and the impact it had and either prepares the reader for a scene change or guides them towards the next scene. If there is any follow-on from the scene that is not immediate (ie it comes later in the story), the conclusion should hint that there is more to come, but not just yet. This keeps the reader interested and eager to read on. It also allows them to engage their imagination.

CHARACTERS

Remember you and the other people in your autobiography are characters. Yes, you are real people, but to your reader (even if they know you well) you are a character. So make sure you give physical descriptions of each person, as well as putting across their personality by showing how each character interacts with you and other people. Put your own personality across by letting the reader know how you feel and what you think. Try the exercise on page 92 to really bring yourself (and others) as characters to life.

A wonderful example of well-developed characters is Hugh Lunn's parents in Over The Top With Jim. These are real people – his parents – but they are also colourful, three dimensional, entertaining characters that could be in any fiction novel. Almost any reader would feel that they have met a Fred or an Olive in their life somewhere (particularly those of similar age to Hugh).

When dealing with characters in your story, remember one of the golden rules of writing – 'show don't tell'. This simply means that you shouldn't just narrate your story in the equivalent of a monotone by telling the reader what happened. You want you reader to be able to use their own imagination and get involved in the story, rather than being directed along in a straight line with no room for interpretation.

Use your characters to show how the story happened. One of the simplest ways to do this it to use dialogue, rather than just dictating events as you remember them.

Here are a couple of examples:

> Telling: Dad told me to go to my room.
> Showing: 'Go to your room now!' Dad said.
> Telling: I told Mum what happened at school.
> Showing: 'Mum, you won't believe what happened at school,' I said.

Remember when you are writing in first person (as almost all autobiographies are written) you can only say for sure what you think and feel, not how other characters do. You can say what you *believe* they think/feel or you can quote how they *said* they think/feel, but you can't get in the head of another character.

If you are able to speak to other characters (family members for example) about incidents you are writing about, you will be able to find out what they did think/feel at the time and you can use this information. Just be sure to explain *how* you know.

USE OF SENSES

Another important thing is to engage all the senses when describing people, places and events in your story. So that means sight, smell, taste, touch and hearing.

Remember that description can make or break a story. Somebody could talk about going on safari in Africa and make in sound very dull if they don't describe it well. On the other hand, another person could write about doing the washing up and make it sound enthralling because of the way they have engaged the senses.

As well as describing physical surroundings you should also talk about things like smells, temperature, weather and noise (or lack thereof). How did you feel at the time – happy, sad, annoyed, depressed, rebellious, guilty, apprehensive or scared? What thoughts were going through your mind? How did you feel physically – energetic, excited, ill, stomach churning? Was it a hot summer's night where there was absolutely no breeze or a cold, bleak winter's day? Can the reader hear the slam of desks in a classroom or taste the sour, sun-warmed milk you had to drink each morning at little lunch?

Keep in mind that you don't have to use a lot of words to describe something well – rather than listing six words that mean roughly the same thing, choose one or two that really bring your story to life. Use a thesaurus to help you use a wide variety of descriptive words.

KEEP A GOOD PACE

Try and keep a good pace and rhythm to your story, even if it involves a lot of sadness and hardship. You don't want to lose your reader in a quagmire of despair. Be conscious of including lighter moments to give your reader a breather and prevent emotional overload. You don't have to tell jokes or try to be overtly funny, just add in at least some things that will make your readers smile.

Even if you have lived a very difficult life, presumably you are telling your story as an inspiration to others that you can overcome hardship. Using humour, even amidst difficult subject matter is an effective way to do this.

Another way to change pace is to include suspenseful and dramatic moments, as well as the more run of the mill events. Almost everybody has got at least a few of these in their life experience.

To gain maximum impact build up some suspense rather than just launching right into the story about the time your car almost slid over a steep embankment or you nearly drowned at the beach. Get the reader onto the edge of their seat before you reveal what happened. You don't want too many of these moments (otherwise it's exhausting to read!) but a few well-placed ones within the story will keep things interesting.

HOW MUCH EXPLANATION DO I NEED?

This can be a hard thing to judge. For example, you might have lived on the land most of your life and will inevitably talk about things that were very familiar to you and to others from the bush, but they wouldn't make much sense to a city person. Or perhaps you were born in another country and recalling your childhood will involve unfamiliar traditions, words, places or objects. Maybe your job involved a lot of technical terms that people outside your particular industry wouldn't have heard of.

A good way to test if you have included too many unfamiliar things is to get somebody else (with a different background to you) to read it and to ask their opinion. Make a note of the things that they think needed more explanation. Obviously you don't want to have to explain every little detail, but you do want your readers to be able to follow the story.

If you think further explanation is necessary, there are a few ways you can provide it for your readers.

➢ Just explain each different thing as part of your story. This isn't a bad thing in itself, but it can take away from the flow of the story if you have several items to expand on.

➢ Use footnotes (similar to what you see in textbooks etc). A footnote is a small number that goes directly after the particular word or phrase in question. Then at the bottom of the page it prints out in smaller type some more details about what you were talking about. This makes it easy for the reader to check down the bottom if they need more details, but doesn't really interrupt the flow of their reading if they don't.

➢ Create a Glossary. This is a list of words/phrases and their meanings, which is inserted at the back of the book. So if a reader comes across something unfamiliar they can flick to the back and look it up.

Further explanation is something you should leave until you have completed at least one draft. It can be time consuming when you are just trying to get your story down and it will interrupt the flow of your writing. Don't be concerned if you don't feel the need for further explanation within your story – it's just an option for those who know there are unfamiliar terms within their writing.

WHOSE NAMES SHOULD I INCLUDE?

If you are writing your life story as a work of non-fiction, then it should be a truthful account and you should include a declaration that it is in fact so (more about that a bit later). In some circumstances this might include people who may not appear in a very good light.

Whether or not you intend to attempt commercial publication of your work, you should be very careful about including names if the person involved comes across in a way that could be considered as defamatory. Otherwise you could be involved in legal action if your claims cannot be proven. Ask yourself if you are indisputably in the right and have enough evidence to prove it. Also ask yourself why you are so intent on including this person(s) name.

If you still consider this individual to be an important part of the story, you can change their name and any obvious details so that they are not identifiable. (Make sure you disguise their identity well, otherwise they could still pursue legal action). You can indicate that you have not used a real name.

Although most people will be pleased and flattered to be included in your story, it is a courtesy to ask them first if they mind their name being included. This is especially important if you intend to distribute your book outside your immediate family or friendship circle.

I'M STUCK!

You're not alone! Almost every writer feels this way at some point. My first piece of advice would be to put your story away for at least a week, or better still two or three. Have a complete break from it. Try to not even think about it (easier said than done, I know!)

When some time has passed, pull it out again and have another look. Firstly, have you got your basics done? Did you compile a memory notebook and then organise your notes into sections? If not, give it a try – you may be surprised how much it helps. Try the exercises below. They are designed to assist you in building memories and fleshing things out to a level where they are interesting to write about.

➤ Describe something from your childhood (or adulthood) in as much detail as you can. For example, can you describe (or draw) the layout of your family house, childhood bedroom, school classroom, grandparents' house etc? Concentrate on details such as if the walls were painted or wallpapered, what kind of furniture there was and what kind of floor coverings. Where were things stored? Did you have a secret hiding place for your own treasures? Can you draw a rough map of the town that you lived in? Concentrate on details like where particular shops or businesses were and whether or not the streets were paved.

➤ Use a similar technique for events. Describe in as much detail as possible an 'everyday' event such as a day at school, the evening meal at your home, a Sunday church service, a game your played or visiting particular relatives or friends. Try to name as many people as possible and describe them. If describing a family meal or get-together for example, think about where people sat, what clothes they wore, what kind of food there was and what type of linen/crockery your family used. What kind of conversation took place? Were you encouraged to have your say or did you have to keep quiet?

After undertaking one or both of these exercises, go back to a scene you're having difficulty with and rewrite it with the new information in mind. If you have success, try another scene (and so on). Even if you're not quite ready to rewrite scenes, do the exercises anyway as they will be helpful when you are in the right head space.

Hopefully undertaking these exercises has helped your "re-boot" and you can now get back into the swing of writing your story. If you can, then go ahead with it (good luck!). But if you are genuinely bogged down and at the point of giving up altogether, it's time to call in some outside help.

If you can afford to call in a professional, then I encourage you to go ahead. Don't feel like you have failed in some way because you are asking for assistance. (Don't we call in plumbers to fix plumbing problems for example?) If it means your story will get finished and will be better because of the help, it is completely worthwhile. Yes, it will cost you money, but shouldn't any professional be paid for the service they provide?

You may need to go on the internet to find a professional (or check the yellow pages if you're in a capital city or large regional area), but there are many writing coaches/editors out there who specialise in helping people back on track with an incomplete manuscript.

Ideally if you can find somebody local to you, that will make it easier. But most editors will accept a posted or emailed manuscript – which means it doesn't really matter where they're located. As long as you can speak to them on the phone, your geographic location is not a problem. Obviously, you need to look into cost and what level of assistance you need, but most will offer a free quote before they begin. You will need to have your story typed to do this.

If you don't have internet access ask a family member or friend to help you, or failing that go to your local library. Staff there can assist you with internet searching.

If a professional is not an option, don't give up just yet. Another alternative is to join a writer's group (as suggested earlier). Within a writer's group you will find people with various levels of experience and expertise who will be able to give an opinion or perhaps edit and work with you. Or maybe they can refer you to someone else who can help. Often all you need is a pair of outside eyes to give you a boost and get you on your way again.

Check your community paper for details about writer's groups in your area or check at your library. If you can't find one, maybe you could start one up yourself. Do you live in a retirement village? You could probably find at least four or five like-minded fellow residents within your immediate community.

What about undertaking a short course in writing? TAFE Open Learning offer writing courses that can be completed via correspondence, as do several other private colleges. Some universities run day or weekend courses specifically for people writing their life story. Some also allow you to undertake writing subjects from within a degree, without having to complete the degree (although this can be expensive). University of the Third Age (U3A) run writing courses (check if there's a branch in your area). Maybe there is a day/evening course in your area at your community centre or senior citizens group? Again, check with your library if you're not sure where to search out details of such organisations.

You can also ask a family member or friend to help. Even if you can get somebody to read your manuscript for you and offer an opinion, that is a start. Just discussing your story with someone outside it can give you a fresh perspective. Even if you have to put it aside for six months or a year, don't ever throw it away. You've started it and with the right direction you can finish it. You never know when you might come across somebody who is able to help you.

In Conclusion.....

Eventually you will get to the point where you are ready to finish the writing of your story. This is an exciting milestone! Even though you will now have to spend time editing, the fact you have worked your way through your first draft is very significant. Well done! Psychologically reaching the conclusion is also very important. I always say it is easier to play around with something you have written, rather than staring at a blank page. Your mindset really does shift once you feel like you're on the home straight. Like writing your introduction, looking at other autobiographies will give you plenty of ideas about how you can conclude your own story.

Most people end their autobiography at the 'present day' ie. at the point they finish writing. Some choose a significant birthday or other family event and others just choose the day they finish writing. If you choose to end your story at a particular point in time (for example ten years earlier), then you could consider an epilogue – which is simply a brief summary outlining what has happened in your life since that time. An epilogue is useful if you have written a memoir that only covered a certain period of your life. Hugh Lunn did this in *Over The Top With Jim*, as it ended when he was eighteen.

Like any story, there should be an attempt to 'wrap up' what you have spoken about in your autobiography. Some authors like to give a summary of their life and what they think have been the highlights/lowlights and the most important lessons they have learned. Others may share some of their own philosophies. Most people give a brief idea of what they would still like to accomplish in their life in the immediate (or distant) future.

As with your introduction, you don't have to get it perfect on your first try. Get something down to begin with and come back to it as you edit and rework it as many times as you need to.

MAKING AN ORAL RECORDING

If you really don't like to write or know that you don't write well getting your story down on paper can be a real challenge. Maybe your formal education was only brief or English is not your first language. Perhaps you are physically incapacitated and simply unable to write legibly (or type). Don't give up just yet! Recording your story orally is a viable alternative.

You can use any kind of recorder to do this – a regular cassette recorder (it doesn't matter how large or how old as long as it records), micro-cassette recorder, digital voice recorder or even the audio recording function on your smartphone or iPad. A regular old school tape recorder is probably simpler for people who are not familiar with newer technology, but digital recorders are also fairly simple to operate. If you are using a digital device of any kind just make sure you keep a backup of all your files in case a file gets accidentally deleted. There is nothing worse than losing hours of spoken information! Ultimately the choice of device is yours – just make it whatever you are comfortable with.

To record orally you need to follow the same steps already discussed. A memory notebook is still necessary (you may need some help to do this if you're incapacitated); you will just be speaking about your experiences rather than writing them down.

Try to make your tapes/files in a reasonably chronological order, or at least speak about one topic at a time, rather than jumping randomly from one thing to another. Have your notes in front of you for each recording session to keep on topic.

➢ Find yourself a quiet place to work uninterrupted and have everything ready in front of you. Know what you intend to speak about for that particular session before you begin. Imagine you are actually conversing with somebody. It will help you get into storytelling mode. Speak clearly (don't mumble) at a steady pace. You don't need to race.

➢ Sometimes you may talk for a long time without a pause and the tape will end before you know it. Other times you might find yourself stopping frequently because you lose your chain of thought. This is all part of the process – when you can't think of what to say, reread you notes and have another go. Maybe take a break for a few minutes or an hour before starting again.

➢ Try to avoid stopping, rewinding and listening to each little section too often. Few people like the sound of their own voice on tape and it can be tempting to cringe at your efforts, erase everything and start again, hoping it will sound better on the next attempt. Fill up a whole tape and then listen to it. If you really think it needs redoing then have another attempt.

➢ Alternatively, you could have a friend or family member interview you. They will need to have a list of questions/topics ready and naturally it should be somebody that you feel comfortable speaking about personal topics with. This can be an effective exercise as the interviewer may often have questions or comments that can add to the story.

➢ Undertake the interviewing over several sessions of around and hour or two. Like writing your story, recording it is not something that can be rushed through (nor should it be). One or two sessions a week over several weeks is a good pace for both you and the interviewer.

➢ Similarly to the writing process, don't worry too much if you leave things out along the way. Just add them into the next tape as you remember them (or perhaps make a written note if you are able to). There is no limit on drafts, so you will be able to slot it into your story in the appropriate place.

Transcribing

Transcribing means to type out an audio recording. Will you be able to do it yourself or will you need help? Perhaps you can recruit a family member or friend to transcribe your tapes to paper (if you are unable to do it yourself). If possible, get them to do it as you complete each recording rather than leaving it all to the end as it is also much less labour intensive if you spread it out. If you don't have somebody who can transcribe your recordings for you, there are professionals who will do it. Get some quotes first to make sure you get the best value for money, but also compare what you are getting. There's no point going cheap if you end up with pages of dot points rather than prose. Maybe get some test pages done first before committing to the whole thing.

There are a couple of ways you can approach transcribing. Some people prefer to just type (or write) each word verbatim as it is spoken, then spend time correcting the grammar and punctuation later. This is definitely the quickest way to record it to paper, but you will have to spend more time editing it down the track.

Another way is to edit as you go. This means you might listen to a section (say a thirty seconds or a minute) and then reword it (if necessary) and construct proper sentences before physically typing it out. So while it takes a lot longer to get it down on paper, there is much less editing to do later.

Whatever method you choose can depend on the speaker too. If they are a fast talker, verbatim can be easier – but if they speak slowly, with precise punctuation, editing as you go is fairly straight forward. Experiment and see which works best for you.

Whichever way you choose, make sure you have a quiet environment to transcribe in and reliable equipment to work with.

HELPING SOMEONE ELSE

You might not be at the point where you are ready to write your own story, but perhaps you are keen to help a parent, grandparent or friend to do theirs. In that case most of the advice given in this book would be the same - it would just have to be applied in a slightly different way.

A memory notebook is still essential. Either get the person to do the notebook themselves or sit with them in several sessions and take notes of the major things they remember. Start with the brainstorming session to really get the ball rolling.

When it comes to getting all the details down, using a recording device is probably the most efficient way. Sit and discuss the points from the memory notebook, making sure you ask questions as you go along to get plenty of information. Then later on make notes from the things that you spoke about. Organise the notes (as described in Part Two) and show them to the person involved. Or maybe you could do this together. Make any additions or adjustments and then you can begin to write the story.

As you write, get the person involved to read what you have written and check that they are happy with how you are writing the story. If they aren't, ask for specific suggestions on what they would like you to change. Discussing the events you are writing about first is a good idea. That way you have an idea what happened in your mind before you begin to write.

Just like writing your own story, your first draft does not have to be perfect. When you get to the editing stage there will be a chance to make improvements. Allow yourself 'time out' breaks, so you don't get frustrated with each other. Even the best of friends or people with a close relationship can get tired of each other when working on something so intense over a period of time.

CHECKLIST FOR PART TWO

★ Complete your first draft from beginning to end (it doesn't matter how roughly) and have at least one attempt at a beginning and conclusion. If you have done an oral recording, your tapes should be transcribed to paper ready for editing.

★ Make a list of words that may be unfamiliar to readers to include in your footnotes or glossary. (Not necessary for everybody).

★ If you already have a list of alterations or additions, have them neatly organised and ready to merge into your manuscript. Check your chronology and make sure you have things in the right order (as best you remember it). Make a note of anything that needs to be moved.

★ If your story is handwritten, I would strongly encourage you at this stage to either type it up yourself or have somebody do it for you. Editing is much easier on typed work. If you are relying on family members or friends to do the typing for you, try and give them your notes at regular intervals so there isn't a giant stack to do all at once. Can you spread it around with different people to share the load? Also consider some kind of reward for their hard work. If it is a teenage grandchild for example, maybe you could give a cash reward – perhaps a set rate per hour or per page? If it's somebody with a young family maybe you could trade babysitting, meal preparation or house cleaning? Other things you could give might be home baked biscuits or cakes, wine or movie tickets.

★ If still haven't finalised your title, spend some time thinking about it and reduce your shortlist to three possibilities.

EDITING YOUR WORK

A day will come when the story inside you will want to breathe on it's own. That's when you will start writing.

Sarah Noffke

EDITING

When you edit you are looking for ways to improve your writing. It is a very important step, but leave it until you have completed your first draft right to the end. Otherwise the flow of your writing will be interrupted, as you try and correct everything in your head before you get it down. Writing is a very creative process whereas editing is technical. So it makes sense to separate the two processes for optimal results.

In my opinion, it is easier to edit well-spaced, typed work (ie double line spacing with three centimetre margins on both sides), as this will allow you to easily mark up your pages. If your eyesight is not the best, have your story typed in a larger font (14 or 16). It can easily be reduced back down later.

To begin:

➢ Make sure you edit in a different coloured pen than what you've written/typed with. Red is the traditional colour, but it doesn't really matter. Just make it highly visible.

➢ Work out a system so you know what each editing mark means. For example, you might circle spelling mistakes, underline grammatical errors; use brackets to indicate a new paragraph and strike a line through something you wish to remove.

➢ Keep a list of your alterations and clearly number each change, so you have an easy-to-follow reference for when you (or your typist) physically make the changes.

➢ You can edit on-screen (if working on a computer), but I recommend doing at least the first major edit on paper as well as the final edit before you completely finish.

Basic Spelling and Grammar Rules

SPELLING

Whether you tackle spelling at the beginning or the end of editing, make sure you spend some time on it. If you are using a computer, spell check makes this task easy. Have your dictionary set to Australian spelling (if possible) to avoid unnecessary flagging of words like colour and realise. Newer versions of Microsoft Word also recognise many place names, once again avoiding unnecessary flagging.

If you are handwriting or using a typewriter, consult a dictionary on any words you are unsure of. There is nothing worse than an interesting story with numerous spelling errors. If spelling is not your strong point, get somebody else to look at it for you and highlight any misspelt words.

Make sure you have used the correct version of there/their, to/too, your/you're etc.

APOSTROPHES AND COMMAS

Many people struggle with the use of apostrophes and commas. They're not as confusing as they seem if you follow the basic rules. Like your times tables, once you learn the rules you will remember them.

<u>The apostrophe should be used:</u>

1. As a contraction – ie to replace omitted letters.

> they are – they're
> could not – couldn't

To show possession – eg. The boy's game. This means the game belongs to the boy.

> Frank's hat
> Jim's trumpet

A common mistake is the use of it's. The only time you use it's is for a contraction - It's a rainy day today.

You don't use it for possession - The dog was chasing its tail.
In plurals, the apostrophe comes after the plural form of the word, which may not necessarily be an 's'.

Children's clothes (clothes belonging to the children).

When a name ends in an s you can either put the apostrophe after the s, or add another s. Whatever way you choose, just make sure you are consistent throughout your writing.

James's car
James' car

2. To avoid confusion.

Dot the i's
Cross the t's

You don't need an apostrophe to indicate a plural. For example, the sentence 'I eat a lot of apples.' does not need an apostrophe. Nor does the abbreviation CDs or the date 1960s.

The comma should be used:

1. Between a list of three or more words, except for the last instance.
    There were small, medium, large and extra-large sizes available.

2. Before a conjunction (but or for).
    I did my best, but the competition was too strong.

3. Where a pause is needed.
    Whatever happens, finish the race.
    As far as I was concerned, it was a dead loss.

4. To avoid confusion.

    To Tom, William was very tall.

5. In dialogue and when quoting direct speech.

    'I can't believe you did that,' said Rebecca.
    Amanda said, 'It was the worst storm I've ever seen.'

6. For conjunctive verbs.

    However, it was a last-ditch attempt and, furthermore, I was too tired.

7. Introductory phrases.

    In general, the children are well behaved.

8. Where the phrase could be in brackets.

    The dog, which was in a cage, still looked scary.

9. Where a phrase adds information.

    Mr Jones, 55, is the oldest in the class.

THE USE OF QUOTATION MARKS (INVERTED COMMAS)

You can either use 'single' or "double" quotation marks to indicate dialogue or make a word or phrase stand out. Double quotation marks used to be the standard in publishing, but single have become more commonplace in recent years. Remember, whichever you choose, be consistent with usage throughout – don't start one way and then change halfway through.

When somebody is speaking, you need to use quotation marks. This can be either through dialogue (conversation) or as a quote of something they have said.

James said, 'I wish we could go home now.'

Michelle jumped in the water. 'It's cold!' she yelled.
'How cold?' replied Susan.
'Freezing,' admitted Michelle.

You don't need quotation marks to indicate your thoughts.

I really wish we could go on holidays, I thought wistfully.

Quotation marks can also be used to make a word or phrase stand out.

I thought it was "the" event of the season.

PARAGRAPHS

Arranging your story into paragraphs is an important part of the editing process. A story that is divided into paragraphs is much more pleasing to the eye than one which is in large, solid blocks of text with no visible white space.

Paragraphs can range from one line to dozens, but the average size is about six or seven lines. A line space (blank line) is then used to indicate a different idea or thought, a change of scene or to show a period of time has passed. Dialogue always has a new line when a different person speaks. Don't get too hung up on the length of your paragraphs, it is not something to spend hours stressing about. You will find that they generally work out pretty evenly.

Indenting (four to five spaces is enough) is used to indicate a new paragraph, but when you leave a line space the first line of that new paragraph is not indented. Sound confusing? Here is an example.

Frank and I had been out all day playing at the river. In those days parents didn't worry about their kids like they do now. As long as we showed up by dark they were content to let us do our own thing.
By four o'clock the weather started to turn bad. The sky grew

grey and the distant rumble of thunder could be heard. It was summer and the storms could be fierce.

'We'd better head home,' Frank suggested.

'Yes,' I agreed.

'Don't forget the fishing rods,' Frank said.

I nodded in agreement and started walking back to the river bank.

The next day it was still raining heavily and my father had a huge list of chores for me to do around the house. I wish I was down at the river again, I thought wistfully.

CHAPTERS

Unless your story is particularly short, you will need to divide it into chapters. Following on from what I said about paragraphs, a story with chapters is much more pleasing to the eye than endless pages with no break. There is no hard and fast rule about how many pages should be in each chapter – just read through your story and work out where a natural place is for a pause is. Each chapter can have a different number of pages, but don't make it a huge variation.

You can either simply number your chapters or give them names if you want to be a little more creative. Named chapters can add colour to a story so they are worth considering. Think about the autobiographies you have read and how each author named their chapters. (They generally relate to an event within those pages.) Then see what you can come up with for your story.

USE OF ABBREVIATIONS

As your life story is an informal document, it is okay to use abbreviations under the right circumstances. For example, when you are using initials to talk about something (an acronym), use the full wording in the first instance with the abbreviation in brackets afterwards eg. University of

Queensland (UQ). After that it is then okay to use the abbreviation as you have explained what it stands for.

The general rule to follow is if the abbreviation is used in everyday language and widely understood, then it is okay to use it. Avoid using abbreviations that may only be used in certain jobs/industries or within your own family or friendship circle. Remember you want your readers to be able to follow the story easily.

When using numbers, there are varying rules. Some people use words up to ten and then figures, others only use figures after one hundred. When you decide which you prefer be consistent throughout.

WHAT ELSE AM I LOOKING FOR?

As well as identifying spelling and grammatical errors, you may need to cut out unnecessary words/sentences or alternatively add in more description and detail. Some of your sentences might be too long. Certain sections may now seem unnecessary or repetitive. You may have some scenes out of order and will need to move them to make your story chronologically accurate (and adjust any surrounding scenes if necessary). You may need to slot in extra scenes.

One of the most effective ways to begin editing is to read your work out loud. This helps you determine if it makes sense. Listen to each sentence as you read it – can you follow it without getting lost? Remember if you stumble over it as you read it aloud, the same will happen to your audience as they read the text.

TENSES

One of the first things you need to check is your tenses. Generally speaking, an autobiography is written in past tense, so you should be referring to everything in that way. Swapping between present and past tenses in a common error for a novice writer.

> My childhood was one long adventure. I really <u>enjoy</u> the day to day work on the farm.

> It should read 'I really <u>enjoyed</u> the day to day work....'

> A new girl joined our class at the beginning of 1950. I think she is beautiful.

> It should be 'I thought she was beautiful' or just 'she was beautiful.'

SENTENCE STRUCTURE

Overall you should try and keep your sentences short and to the point. However, there are times when a longer sentence is needed and that is fine. Just make sure it is correctly punctuated so the reader doesn't get lost within it. (Refer to comma rules on page 57). As I just mentioned read it out loud to see if it makes sense.

Limit your use of words like: quite, a bit, just, that and ly adjectives such as certainly, definitely, really. Look at the two sentences below:

> I certainly thought that it was a really good idea at the time. In fact I was quite definite that it was.

> I thought it was a good idea.

The second sentence says the same thing with less words. As a result, it has more impact and you have not lost any information in this shorter form.

DON'T BE TOO 'WORDY'

More words do not necessarily equal a more interesting story; in fact they usually do the opposite. When an author uses too many words the end result is 'waffle'. Put aside any set ideas that your story has to be a certain number of pages and just see where it takes you. You are much better with a 100-page story written 'tightly' (ie with as few words as possible) than with a 250 page tale full of padding that detracts from the storyline.

The word 'that', in particular, is overused a lot in writing. Of course there are times when it is necessary, but use it sparingly.

> I knew <u>that</u> my parents thought <u>that</u> my boyfriend was rude.

> I knew my parents thought my boyfriend was rude.

Keeping your writing informal also helps to eliminate excess words. Write how you speak.

> I believed it could possibly be true.

> I thought it was true.

Use positive rather than negative statements. It makes a statement or sentence definite and removes unnecessary words.

-ve: I did not remember her birthday.
+ve: I forgot her birthday.

-ve: She was not very often so punctual.
+ve: She was often late.

PASSIVE/ACTIVE VOICE

Where possible use the active voice, rather than the passive. In the active voice, the subject of the sentence acts upon something or someone. In the passive voice, the subject is acted upon.

I was hit by a jolt of panic (passive).
A jolt of panic hit me (active).

The room was lit up by the candle light (passive).
The candle lit up the room (active).

AVOID USING CLICHÉS

They are unnecessary and overused. Instead try to be original in the way you write.

Along the same lines be aware of any words/phrases you have overused in your writing. This may not become apparent until you are at the editing stage. Be aware of any of the following:

At the end of the day…..
Quite frankly……
Nevertheless…..
Fair dinkum……

Of course, there are thousands of others as well. This may be how you speak, but a reader will find them repetitive and annoying. I know I said before you shouldn't be afraid to use your own words and expressions, but like anything moderation is the key. You should aim not to use them more than four or five times throughout the story. If you are using a computer to type your story use the 'find' function to track how many times you may have used a word or phrase.

USE A VARIETY OF VERBS

Verbs are the doing words of your story and give it life. Where possible try to substitute alternatives for everyday words. For example, 'walked' could be sauntered, ambled, scuttled etc. 'Sat down' could be plonked, flopped onto the chair. 'Laughed' could be chortled, giggled, guffawed. Do you get the picture? There are many others you could use as well.

Use a thesaurus or the synonym function on your computer and see how many interesting alternatives you can come up with. Of course, there's nothing wrong with using the everyday words as well, just strike a balance between both to keep your writing more dynamic.

REMOVE UNNECESSARY SCENES

Once you have got the technical side of things sorted out, it's time to go back and do some more pruning of your work. Are there any scenes that don't help move the story along? If so, you should remove them or at least cut them back.

Yes, it is difficult to cut out words that you spent a long time working on initially, but sometimes for the good of the story you have to. Try to be objective about what you would find interesting as a reader. Yes, it might be important to you, but does it belong in a story that you want other people to read (and enjoy)?

Sometimes you don't need to remove a whole scene, just parts of it. Have you spent too long describing someone or something? Are there lines and lines of dialogue that could be condensed down?

Remember, your autobiography is essentially the highlights and lowlights of your life, not every single mundane detail. That's not to say that you can't include day-to-day references (and in fact you should), just don't write pages and pages about them.

GET YOUR CHRONOLOGY RIGHT

As you write, you will probably find parts of your story that are out of order. If your story has been typed on a computer, it is very easy to move things around using the 'cut and paste' function. If you're unsure about exactly when something happened, do a bit of research and see if you can verify it.

If you do move something, make sure that you also adjust the text before and after it. For example, of you talk about your friend Edward in chapter four, but realise you didn't meet him until chapter five, make sure you remove all references of him from chapter four, not just the scene where you introduce him. You don't have to be fastidious about chronology, but for the sake of historical accuracy try and get it as close as possible.

CONFIRM HISTORICAL FACTS AND DATES

If you have been using your memory to cite historical facts or date, you should confirm that they are correct. Some you will know for absolute certain, but some might have become a little bit fuzzy over the passage of time. It doesn't take much effort to check and will show that you have been professional in the way you have approached your life story. Near enough is not good enough!

DOUBLE CHECK ALL NAMES

Even though this is your story and you know the people and places well you have written about, you should double check that you have all names correct. This means both spelling and the actual name itself. You might swear that girl you knew in grade three was called Mary-Ann, but she was actually Mary-Jane. Or you might be fairly sure that little town you visited was called Appletown when it was actually Appleville. This might seem like nit picking, but once again it adds authenticity to your story if you have all the little details correct, as well as the big ones. Besides that, Mary-Jane or a resident of Appleville might read your book and will be annoyed if they aren't correctly portrayed!

USE OUTSIDE EYES

No matter how good your writing skills are, it is very helpful to have somebody else look at your work and offer an opinion and constructive criticism.

There are many ways you can do this. If you can afford to, having a professional editor work on your manuscript is money well spent. Depending on how much you are prepared to spend they will either point out issues that need to be worked on or do the corrections for you. Many people resist the idea of having to spend money on editing, but just like any professional service provider editors spend time and effort on your story and deserve to be paid fairly for their work. Ask for a quote first so you know what it will cost before agreeing to go ahead. If it seems like too much, ask if there is anything you can do first to help reduce the cost. This can be as simple as removing extra spaces or fixing your formatting, but can save you money as it is time that the editor does not have to spend during the job.

Another way is to get somebody you know to edit for you. A teacher or other kind of professional is ideal, or maybe you are acquainted with somebody who has good English skills. Perhaps to save some money you could have them edit it for you first before taking it to a professional.

Whatever level of editing you decide on; it is definitely worthwhile. Even if you are a competent writer and speller, once you have read the text numerous times your mind will start to take shortcuts and not notice small errors like missing/extra words or other little inconsistencies. This is where an outside pair of eyes can be very valuable.

It can be difficult to show something you have written (and sweated over) to another person. Also, it can be difficult to be objective about your own work. But it is something that you must do to make your story as good as it can possibly be.

Ask the editor (whether professional or amateur) to be honest about what they think and be open to the ideas they present. You don't have to take them all on board, but they will almost certainly be worth considering. If you think that the editor has been particularly harsh or unhelpful, find somebody else who can be more constructive.

Remember an editor (whether professional or amateur) is only trying to help you improve your work. It does feel personal because your story is personal – but they are only judging your words, not you as a person. Leave the comments aside for a day or two and then read them again when your ego is not feeling quite so bruised. You will probably find that they don't sting quite so much the second, third and fourth times you read them. Also look for general themes within your work. For example, the editor might mention that you overuse certain words or use passive voice instead of active. Taking that on board, go through your entire manuscript just focussing on that one thing before moving onto the next.

Editing is not a once only process. You will probably edit your story at least five or six times (and some sections even more). If you are working on a computer, you can do some editing on-screen, but you should also edit your hard (printed out) copy. You will be amazed how many extra things you notice when you work from a printed copy compared to screen.

Each time you make corrections, have them worked into your typed copy, then reprint it and begin the editing process again (although not immediately). Work through your whole manuscript each time – even if you're sure there's nothing more to change in certain sections. Sometimes you can have a flash of insight about changing something or you will pick up a small error on the tenth or twentieth read through.

A good tip is to leave several days between each edit (or even a week or two if possible). If you continually re-read your work for days on end you will get so sick of it that you might lose focus. Under these circumstances your editing will not be as effective and you will miss errors and be less inclined to come up with improvements.

Editing can be frustrating and tedious at times, but ultimately it will improve your story significantly.

CHECKLIST FOR PART THREE

★ Thoroughly edit your work at least four or five times (and/or have somebody else do it for you). Ensure that your story is as perfect as you can make it before moving onto the presentation stage. Have you:

- Corrected all spelling and grammatical errors
- Removed any unnecessary words/paragraphs or scenes
- Ensured you haven't overused particular words or phrases
- Divided your story into paragraphs and chapters
- Checked that your chronology and any historical facts are correct
- Completed all insertions/deletions and moved any scenes that were out of place

★ Re-work your opening and closing paragraphs until you are completely happy. Have you set the scene adequately in your introduction and wrapped things up in the conclusion?

★ Finalise your title and cover design. If you are still struggling to come up with a title, ask other people for ideas. In the end there is nothing wrong with calling it 'My Story' if you can't come up with anything else that captures you.

PRESENTING YOUR STORY

Start writing no matter what.
The water does not flow until
the tap is turned on.

Louis L'Amour

FINISHING TOUCHES

You are almost there! Once the editing is done, you can move onto the more enjoyable (and exciting) part – adding those finishing touches that will add a touch of professionalism to your story and really make it official.

PHOTOS AND OTHER MEMENTOES

If possible, include photographs to enhance your story. They add so much to the finished product and serve as a great reference point to help the reader visualise some of the people and places you are talking about. (Now that you have sorted your photos and sourced copies of photos from other people (as per page 23), you will have a great range to choose from). Depending on how you are going to present your book these photos can be printed in black and white or in colour. Most people group their photographs together in several pages rather than inserting them within the story. Make sure you include a description for each photo.

It is also possible to include other mementos like copies of letters, cards, pages from schoolbooks and certificates. These can be scanned like a photo and inserted in the story.

You might also like to include a favourite quote, poem, song lyrics or something similar. If you do this, however, you need to acknowledge where it came from. If it is from a person you know, simply ask their permission to use it and then state this either within your story or at the end.

If you are using things that have been previously published (for example an excerpt from a book or a photograph) you should get permission from the publisher to include it in your story (if this is possible). You should state the full publishing details and where it originally appeared. If you can't get permission from the publisher (if the book is out of print for example or the publisher no longer exists), give as many details as you can, making sure you state it is not your own work/image. If you don't do this, you are breaching copyright.

COPYRIGHT

In Australia, you are automatically granted copyright for anything you write. You do not need to register anywhere. Simply include the © symbol after your name and the year on the inside of your cover, or on page 2 (the back of your title page).

DEDICATION

When reading your autobiographies (and other books) you would have noticed that some of them have a dedication to a person (or several people) or even to a place. A dedication is not mandatory – if you don't want to have one you don't have to. On the other hand, if you have somebody or something you want to dedicate your story to, just write it on a page by itself before the body of your story begins. A dedication is generally quite short – if it goes beyond a few lines, it is probably better to include it as an acknowledgement (see below).

FOREWORD

A foreword is normally written by somebody else and introduces you and your story to the reader. It is often somebody well known who wants to show they have a connection with the author and are putting their name behind the book. Even if you only intend to distribute your book among family and friends, a foreword/introduction can be a nice touch if you know somebody who would like to write one for you. Maybe it might be a local identity or you may know a celebrity or sporting star who wants to lend their name to your masterpiece. Or it could just be a friend or family member who wants to write a foreword for you. The Foreword goes after the dedication (if you have one) but before the main body of the story.

ACKNOWLEDGEMENTS

The acknowledgement page (or pages) is a great way to thank people who have helped you, or perhaps inspired you to write your story. Obviously, you don't need to go overboard and thank hundreds of people, but try to include anybody who has been of help – this can range from your children/grandchildren helping you with computer issues, your friends/family who reminisced with you and/or shared stories, the local library for assisting you with research, anybody who has provided photographs etc, etc. Most people who undertake a life story need help and support, so it is nice to take some time and space to thank those who gave it to you. The acknowledgements can either go at the front (after the dedication but before the main body of the story) or at the end (after the conclusion).

DECLARATION

It is not mandatory to have a declaration, but it's not a bad idea. In your declaration, you are simply stating that your story is a truthful account of your life as you remember it. You can acknowledge that details may not be 100% accurate – but they are as close as you can make them.

Many authors may say something like … 'any errors are unintentional, but I accept they may exist within the various stories within these pages...' or something along those lines. Once again, you can look at the various autobiographies you have read and see how other authors phrase it.

If you have chosen to leave out things that may have caused controversy, you can add a statement indicating that. For example – 'I have chosen not to elaborate on some life events that may cause strife to myself or others. Those secrets will just have to remain with me…'

HOW DO I SET IT OUT?

If you are self-publishing, technically you can set your book out however you like. However, most people like to follow the industry standard for a published book. It adds an extra touch of professionalism and it's a good idea if you want to sell your book. There is no absolute rule for set up as different publishing houses sometimes vary, but this is generally how it goes:

TITLE

The first page is your title page. It is the title of your book (in a large font) and your name (as the author). Some books have an extra title page, but for the purposes of your book it is not really necessary.

PAGE 2

Page 2 contains the publishing information and is generally always on the back of the title page. This states where and when the book was published (even if you're only doing a DIY print on the computer you can still list that you published it in your town/state and the year). It also includes a paragraph about your work being copyright (with the © symbol) and states that your book cannot be reproduced without your consent. Check any published book to get an idea how to word it. Page 2 also includes your ISBN (if you have one).

DEDICATION ETC

As discussed above the dedication, acknowledgements and declaration (if you have one) go next.

TABLE OF CONTENTS

This is an option but not mandatory. It is simply a list of the chapters/sections of your story and may include photos and other mementoes, glossary (if applicable) and any other additions.

FOREWORD

This is the final addition before the actual story begins. To get a good visual of how to set it out just look at a commercially published book and follow their set up.

PRESENTATION

Once you have gotten your story to the stage where you are happy with it and are ready for others to read it, then it is time to decide how to present it. Presentation is very important to make your story appealing to readers and the good new is that presenting your story in a professional looking way does not have to cost a lot of money.

DIY PRESENTATION

Do It Yourself (DIY) presentation does not have to look cheap and unprofessional. In fact thanks to computer technology, it can be just the opposite.

At the very least you should get your story typed up on a computer. Word processors have excellent features, which allow them to set out a story in a very professional looking way. You can choose a particular font (typeface), how large the print will be and the way that you want your story set out.

If you don't have access to a computer yourself, ask around. Almost every family today has at least one computer and your adult children or grandchildren will almost certainly have enough expertise to type it up for you. If not family, ask friends. They may have family members who can do it, or maybe they're computer literate themselves. If that's still not an option, there are typing services who will type it for you at a fairly reasonable cost. Maybe you could consider completing a computer course so you can do it yourself?

You can use a typewriter if you really want to, but there is a lot less flexibility about what you can do with the text compared to a computer. Having your story on computer also makes it easy to move and re-order text and change the layout as many times as necessary until you're happy with it. This is particularly helpful when you are doing the final edits and there are just minor details to be changed. If you have opted to include photographs and other mementoes, they can be scanned into the document and set out as you desire. Your cover can also be easily designed on a computer, with little artistic experience required.

The average computer printer today will produce a very professional looking document. Photos print out clearly too, even on plain paper. Choose good quality paper and cardboard for your covers. If you like you can use special photo paper for photos. Once the document is printed out, having it bound (with wire or comb binding) is inexpensive. This can be done at numerous print/copy shops such as Office Works.

Before printing numerous copies of your story, have a few test runs. Get different people to have a look at it and tell you honestly what they think. This includes the written story itself and the presentation. Ask them if there was anything they didn't understand or if they felt more or less detail was required. See if they found it easy to follow. Did they think there were too many photographs or too few? See what they think about the size and style of the typeface. Use the feedback to make any necessary changes and then print as many as you require. You can do more later if necessary.

SELF-PUBLISHING

Self-publishing has come a long way in the last decade or so. While it used to be very expensive, thanks once again to computer technology, it has become much more affordable – which makes is a viable option for the average person. Many people are using the option of self-publishing their work these days.

When you self-publish, you have your story printed by a professional printer into a hardback or paperback book that looks just like a commercially released book. The difference is that you pay the printing costs yourself. Also, you make all the decisions about the content of the book. Basically, you can get anything printed, as long as you pay for it.

If you are prepared to outlay the money to self-publish, you should definitely have your work edited first. Some self-publishing companies can refer you to an editor, or you can find one yourself – but it is money well spent. Don't you agree it is off-putting as a reader to come across mistakes in a book? You've put a lot of hard work into telling your story, so you should present it in its best possible light.

These days you don't have to have a large minimum print run if you use the cheaper option of Print On Demand (POD). In fact, you can print as few as one book – with the option of having more printed if required. This is ideal if you want to test your market first, before committing to a larger print run. Or even if you just want to check how the finished product looks (layout, font etc). Print on Demand uses a process similar to photocopying rather than using a traditional offset printing press. In all honesty unless you use a magnifying glass to examine the finished print it is almost impossible to tell the difference between a POD and traditionally printed book. The cost per book varies, but on average a 300-page book (6 x 9 inch) would be between $5 - $7. This may then decrease if you have a larger number of copies.

Whether you choose POD or a traditional print, you can choose the size of your book, binding type, the kind of cover, paper quality etc. All these elements can be tailored to your budget. Shop around and get several itemised quotes before you make a decision. There are many POD companies out there these days, use the internet to find them. Most will accept your manuscript in word format and do and rest for you. POD also allows you to make changes to your book if you need to without incurring a large cost. (Most companies charge a small fee only). Ingram is one of the best-known POD companies (with a printing facility in Melbourne) and is a good place to start.

Once your book is printed, you might like to try and sell it. You could approach your library, the local paper, small bookstores or many other avenues to give it some exposure. Selling on-line is also a great way to distribute your book (either on a site like Ebay, or you could get your own website). Call on family members to help or check with your self-publishing company if they offer a distribution service (many of them do). For a percentage of your sale price, a distributor will approach bookstores with your book and try to persuade them to buy it. If you are not an aggressive marketer, a distributor can really help to get your book out into the marketplace.

It will take time and energy to market your book yourself, but if you generate some sales, the results are well worth it.

E-BOOKS

E-books have exploded over the past decade as more and more people have started using e-readers (Amazon Kindle is perhaps the best known). Whether or not you personally prefer a "real" book, making your book available as an e-book is a great idea. The good news is it will not cost you very much to have your existing book manuscript converted to e-book format. You can then email it to people if you like or you can have it listed for sale on such sites as Amazon or iBooks.

You can either set your e-book up yourself or use a company that will take care of everything for you (for a fee). One such site is www.australianebookpublisher.com.au. The great thing about e-books is that there are no ongoing costs involved in printing and storage and you can update, correct or change your book easily whenever you like. It is also instantly accessible for anybody who wants to buy it.

CAN I GET COMMERCIALLY PUBLISHED?

That is a good question! To be realistic only a handful of hopefuls get their work published commercially. That doesn't mean that other stories aren't interesting or worthy of publishing it just means that the decision makers at that time don't believe the story in question will make them a good financial return. On the other hand, there are always publishers on the lookout for interesting and inspiring stories from unknown people, so it is not impossible.

If you truly believe your story has a chance to be published, then you should pursue it. A good first step is to have your manuscript assessed by a professional assessor. For a fee, they will give an opinion on whether they think your manuscript has commercial potential. Generally, they also provide a report offering suggestions about how it could be improved to make it more marketable. If they think it has real potential, they may even refer you straight to a publisher.

If you're assessment is promising, it's up to you to seek out a publisher. Be smart about how you approach them. Do some research on different publishing companies and target those that deal in autobiographies. There's no point sending a letter to every publishing house in Australia if only 20% of them publish autobiographies or memoirs.

Consider smaller and less well-known companies. Research the best way to approach a publisher and make sure you have a well-written, correctly presented covering letter. Get somebody to help you if necessary. Be prepared for rejection letters, but don't be disheartened. Remember you can always self-publish and make your way into the mainstream market. Many well-known authors start out that way.

You have got nothing to lose by having a go at the publishing market. It is better than wondering 'what if'.

In Conclusion

Congratulations – you did it! If you followed this book right through, you progressed from having a desire (which may have seemed out of reach) to producing your very own life story in print. That is an amazing achievement and you should be very proud of yourself.

For those of you who have struggled along the way and maybe given up – don't! Try to find someone who can help you get your story finished. You started it and I know you want to finish it. Maybe read this book again and see if you can gain some new inspiration along the way. If you have to, put the whole thing aside for a while and come back to it later.

I wish you the very best of luck with getting your book to your desired reading audience - whether it be your immediate family only, your family and friends or out in the commercial marketplace. Remember it doesn't really matter how many people read it, as long as at least one person enjoys it and gains something from the words you have written, then the journey has been worthwhile.

The final section of this book contains some further information that may help you. It includes extra writing exercises, as well as further information about starting your own writers group, self-publishing and using the internet. There is also a list of autobiographies that you might like to read to help and inspire you as you work on yours.

If you have any questions or comments regarding this book please email me at: info@helenmckenna.com.au. I welcome your feedback.

CHECKLIST FOR PART FOUR

★ Finalise your dedication, acknowledgements, declaration and foreword/introduction (if any of these are applicable). Also finalise any photos and other mementoes you are including.

★ Make sure you have acknowledged any photographs, quotes or other written work that are not your own.

★ When you are deciding how to present your book thoroughly research each option first. Self-publishing may seem financially out of reach, but is there some way you can make it happen? Could you forgo a luxury somewhere else to facilitate it? See if any family members would be willing to chip in to raise the money (maybe in lieu of birthday or Christmas presents?).

★ If you are going to self-publish have your work edited by an outsider. If not a professional, at least somebody with superior written English skills.

★ Also if you self-publish, make sure you have an ISBN (International Standard Book Number). This 13-digit number uniquely identifies books and book-like products published internationally. Many self-publishing companies will obtain this for you (see Part Five for further details). You will also need to lodge a copy of your book with the National Library in Canberra and the State library in your home state.

EXTRA INFORMATION

If the book is true it will
find an audience that is
meant to read it.

Wally Lamb

LIST OF AUTOBIOGRAPHIES/MEMOIRS

Below is a list of autobiographies and memoirs to get you started. It is not an exhaustive list, there are literally thousands of others out there – but it is a good place to start from. The majority of them are Australian, but you don't have to limit your reading to Australian titles.

Try your library first as they will have many of these titles or you can try bookstores, second hand bookstores, op shops or on-line sites like Ebay (who will often have cheap second-hand books).

★ Over The Top With Jim – Hugh Lunn
★ Head Over Heels – Hugh Lunn
★ From strength to strength - Sara Henderson
★ Never Tell Me Never – Janine Shepherd
★ A Long Way Home – Saroo Brierley
★ This Is Me – Ian Thorpe
★ Cliffy: The Cliff Young Story – Julietta Jamieson
★ The Long Road To Overnight Success – Shane Jacobsen
★ The Happiest Refugee – Anh Do
★ Mao's Last Dancer – Li Cunxin
★ Steve and Me – Terri Irwin
★ Angela's Ashes – Frank McCourt
★ 30 Days in Sydney - Peter Carey
★ A Passion for life - Paul Brock
★ A fortunate life - AB Facey
★ After Bali - Jason McCartney
★ To Have And To Hold – Walter Mikac
★ A Passionate Life – Ita Buttrose
★ Allan Border: An Autobiography - Allan Border
★ Anything But: An Autobiography - Richie Benaud

- ★ Barry Humphries: My Life as Me - Barry Humphries
- ★ Beneath Whose Hand - R.M. Williams
- ★ Between The Lines: My Story Uncut - Jason Donovan
- ★ Born to Win: a lifelong struggle to capture the America's Cup – John Bertrand
- ★ Caddie: A Sydney Barmaid - Caddie
- ★ Treading Water – Tracey Wickham
- ★ Cathy: Her Own Story - Catherine Freeman
- ★ Dawn: One Hell of a Life – Dawn Fraser
- ★ Dawn French: Dear Fatty - Dawn French
- ★ Diary of a dropout: One Australian's amazing saga through his years of life - Russell Frank Atkinson
- ★ Don't let her see me cry - Helen Barnacle
- ★ Don't Fence Me In - Wendy McCarthy
- ★ Every Goose A Swan: An Australian Autobiography - Robert Langdon
- ★ Fishing In The Styx - Ruth Park
- ★ Fred Hollows: The Updated Autobiorgaphy - Peter Corris
- ★ Golden Girl - Betty Cuthbert
- ★ Ugly – Robert Hoge
- ★ Out of The Shadows – Wally Lewis
- ★ Hands and Heals - Ian Healy
- ★ Hayden - Bill Hayden
- ★ I can jump puddles - Alan Marshall
- ★ Lillee: Over and Out - Dennis Lillee
- ★ Lionheart - Jesse Martin
- ★ Long Walk To Freedom: The Autobiography of Nelson Mandela - Nelson Mandela
- ★ Losing My Virginity - Richard Branson
- ★ Lost In The Himalayas - James Scott and Joanne Robinson

- ★ Maggie - Maggie Tabberer
- ★ Mem's The Word - Mem Fox
- ★ My Other World - Margaret Whitlam
- ★ My Place - Sally Morgan
- ★ My Regards to Broadway: A Memoir - James Fairfax
- ★ My Story - Dannii Minogue
- ★ My Story - Nova Peris
- ★ My Way or The Highway - Stan and Marcella Zemanek
- ★ Never Say Die - Chris O'Brien
- ★ Newk - John Newcombe
- ★ On A Wing and a Prayer - David Campese
- ★ Parcel Arrived Safely: Tied With String: My Autobiography - Michael Crawford
- ★ Parky: My Autobiography - Michael Parkinson
- ★ Passages of time - Mary Edgeworth David
- ★ Pat Cash: Uncovered - Pat Cash
- ★ Plumb Crazy - Gwen Plumb
- ★ Raelene: Sometimes Beaten, Never Conquered - Raelene Boyle
- ★ Ray: Stories of My Life - Ray Martin
- ★ Recollections of an Unreasonable Man: From the Beat to the Bench – Don Stewart
- ★ Romulus: My Father - Raymond Gaita
- ★ Love, Sweat and Tears – Zelie Bullen
- ★ Shane Warne: My Autobiography - Shane Warne
- ★ Since I was a Princess - Jacqueline Pascarl
- ★ Slide Rule : The Autobiography Of An Engineer - Nevil Shute
- ★ Speaking For Myself: The Autobiography - Cherie Blair
- ★ Stagestruck - Val Jellay
- ★ Survival – Stuart Diver
- ★ Tell me I'm here - Anne Deveson

- ★ The Divine mistake: An Autobiography - Theresa Byrnes
- ★ The Naked Truth - Graeme Blundell
- ★ The Paperboy's War - Ted Egan
- ★ The Quest For Grace - Manning Clark
- ★ Unbearable Lightness – Portia de Rossi
- ★ Heart of Stone – Michael Chamberlain
- ★ The autobiography of the woman the Gestapo called the white mouse – Nancy Wake
- ★ The cattle king - Sir Sidney Kidman - Ion L Idriess
- ★ Through my eyes - Lindy Chamberlain-Creighton
- ★ True Colours - Adam Gilchrist
- ★ True Spirit - Jessica Watson
- ★ Tumble Turns - Shane Gould
- ★ Under The Southern Cross - David Boone
- ★ Through The Farm Gate – Angela Goode
- ★ Kath's Miracle – Kathleen Evans
- ★ An Outback Life – Mary Groves
- ★ Shadows of War on The Brisbane Line – Graham Smith
- ★ What It Takes – Mark Bouris
- ★ Now I Can Dance – Tina Arena
- ★ The Voice – Ray Warren
- ★ Hey True Blue – John Williamson
- ★ The Climb – Geraldine Doogue
- ★ I'm Talking – Kate Cebrano
- ★ Making Gravy – Paul Kelly
- ★ A Simpler Time – Peter Fitzsimons
- ★ Love, Sweat and Tears – Zelie Bullen
- ★ How I Met Your Father – Aminah Hart
- ★ Reckoning – Magda Szubanski
- ★ All For My Children – Sally Faulkner

USING THE INTERNET

The idea of using the internet can strike fear into the hearts of some people. As I said in the beginning I am not trying to push you into using technology if you don't want to. And I'm not saying that the internet is not without its downsides. However, when it comes to finding information, it is an amazing tool. For historical facts, you can find almost anything on the internet – dates, people, places – the list is endless. You just type in a keyword or two and you will have a huge barrage of information at your fingertips. Have you ever considered doing a short course in using the internet? Most libraries run them regularly. Of course, if you have someone you can ask to do internet searches for you, then you're all set.

Another way the internet is helpful when writing your life story is to help you find people who can help – this includes editors, publishers, writing coaches or even forums or chat rooms where you can link up with other people writing their life story and exchange information with them. Even if you don't use the internet directly, the information you get can be very helpful. For example, you might ask somebody to find a list of editors/writing coaches and just use their phone numbers to call them or write to them at their postal address. This allows you to speak to anybody Australia wide, rather than just your own immediate area. Can you imagine how long it would take to search every telephone directory in Australia for information that is available within seconds on-line?

The internet can also be useful is to sell your book. You can list it on any number of on-line sites (Ebay for example) or you could even set up your own site (or have somebody do it for you) to promote your book and get it out in the public eye. Don't be afraid of the internet – instead use it to your advantage.

SETTING UP A WRITER'S GROUP

If you can't find a suitable writer's group in your area, why not set up your own? It's not as hard as it sounds. All you need is a group of like-minded people, a place to meet and plenty of enthusiasm. As I mentioned previously, if you live in a retirement village it's almost too easy. Put a notice on the noticeboard and wait for others to come to you.

Otherwise you can place an ad in your local community newspaper (most do this for free), in your neighbourhood centre, library, bookstore, in the newsletter of any organisations you belong to or on the radio or TV (most offer a free service for community advertisements). You can also use a website like Meetup.com, or start a Facebook Group. Emphasise that anybody of any skill level is welcome and that all you need is a desire to improve your writing skills and discuss writing. If you want to, you could make your group specifically for people wanting to write their life story.

Allow a few weeks for the message to get out there and people to respond and then plan your first meeting. Even if you only have three or four to begin with, it's a start. In fact a small group like that can be just as productive as a large one. If you're not in a retirement village or going through your community centre, arrange your first meeting in a public place like a coffee shop or a park. This allows everybody to meet each other on neutral ground.

You might feel a bit nervous before your first meeting, but so will everybody else. As well as introducing yourselves, you will need to sort out some administrative tasks. For example, how often do you want to meet, at what time and more importantly where? If you don't have access to a meeting room or hall (this is great if you can manage it), perhaps there might be someone who is willing to host the meetings in their home? Or several people could take turns? Some libraries have meeting rooms or you could have it in a coffee shop (as long as it's not too noisy).

You will also need to decide how long you want each meeting to go for and if you want refreshments to be served – if you do you will need to organise a roster and a gold coin donation to cover costs. Or maybe each person could bring something.

Next you will need to decide what format you want your meetings to take. Do you want to adopt the formal meeting style of keeping minutes etc or are you happy with a more casual approach? Even if you want to be casual, you will need some kind of structure. Maybe each member could take turns running a meeting – for example choosing a writing exercise to do and discuss or choosing a topic to have a discussion about. If you have chosen to focus your group on writing your life story you could use this book (or another if you prefer) to work through and compare notes along the way.

Whatever ever format you end up undertaking, make sure that everybody gets a chance to have their say and that each member feels comfortable expressing themselves. No doubt there will be a large range of writing abilities within your group, but even those least skilled should feel confident sharing ideas and written work, knowing that they will receive only constructive criticism and positive suggestions. There will probably be group members who prefer to sit back and listen rather than actively contribute and that is okay too. It can take a lot of courage to share something personal and it may take them a while to get to that point. Encourage people to contribute, but don't force them. Nobody likes to be pressured into things they aren't comfortable with.

Maybe your group could put together a compilation of stories as a project? It is a great shared goal to work towards, as well as each individual's life story.

GETTING YOUR OWN ISBN

If you would like to get your own ISBN, Thorpe-Bowker handle ISBN distribution in Australia. Their website is: www.myidentifiers.com.au or phone: (03) 8517 8333. It is a good idea to get an ISBN as it makes it much easier to have your book listed for sale and to be placed into libraries around Australia (or the world for that matter). It is a bit like a fingerprint for your book. There is a one-time cost involved.

EXTRA WRITING EXERCISES

These exercises would be ideal for using in a writer's group or you can just do them yourself.

DECIDING ON A TITLE

List the titles of the autobiographies you have read and see if you can determine how each author came up with their name. This should be fairly easy to do (especially if it is called My Story!). For those that have not used My Story/My Life in the title is it something personal or something that a whole generation of people might relate to? Either option is fine, however if you are an unknown author using a title that is eye-catching will draw readers in.

Now go through each section of your story and select one possible title relating to something in that particular section. For example if one of your sections is school days it could be something like: 'Hopscotch, Elastics and Daisy Chains' Make a list of the possible titles and rank them from best to worst. Now set the list aside and come back to it a week later. Rank the titles again – did you rank them the same this time? Would you consider the one you ranked your favourite as the actual title of your book? If not, try the following exercise.

Is there something unique about you and/or your life that would make a catchy title? Do you have a favourite saying or philosophy or could you use a play on your name? I know of a man named Frank who used the title 'Quite Frankly' and a woman named Raylene who used 'A Little Ray of Sunshine'. Do you have a nickname that would make a fun title?

Repeat the instructions above (making a list and ranking). If you're still not happy repeat one or both of these exercises or ask around and see if anyone else has a title you like. As I said previously using My Life or My Story is perfectly fine.

WORKING ON YOUR INTRODUCTION

List five autobiographies you have read, then study the introduction for each one carefully. For each author write a brief summary of how they have begun their story then answer the following questions:

- Has the writer drawn you in with their first paragraph? Did you feel the desire to keep reading?
- Has the writer set the scene in time and place? (ie do you know where they are and what era?
- Has the author used a prologue? If so how and where?
- Did you like the intro? Why or why not?
- Give it a rating out of ten.

When you have completed the exercise for all five books (you can do more if you like), make a summary of the good points and any bad points from any of the intros. Make a note of anything you would like to emulate in your introduction.

CONCLUSION

Repeat the same for the conclusion, changing the questions to these:

- Has the writer wrapped up their story, rather than just ended it abruptly?
- Have they given any personal philosophies or words of advice to their readers?
- Do you feel like you know and understand the person better after reading their story?
- Has the writer used an epilogue? Did it give enough info about what has happened since the story ended?

Note: you are not trying to copy somebody else's work, just gaining ideas in style and theme.

VERB VARIETY

For the list of everyday verbs below, come up with at least two alternatives for each (more if you can manage it).

Sat   Laugh   Jump   Ran   Walk   Smile

Go through your story and replace the everyday with an alternative where possible.

I REMEMBER

Pick something from your life – eg a person, a day, an event and write for fifteen minutes, not getting too concerned about style or grammar – just write whatever you can think of about the topic. Some examples could be: the school library, the spooky house in the next street, my grandfather, the person I sat next to in grade three, my first cricket match, swimming lessons, my childhood friend Bob…….etc, etc. When you have finished see if there is anything useful you can use in your story. (Chances are there will be).

You can do the same thing but using the phrase **I Don't Remember**. Of course, the more you focus on what you can't remember about someone or something the more things you will come up with. Once again you need to keep writing for fifteen minutes. This can be very useful for digging up information you're sure that you have forgotten.

CHARACTER STUDY

As discussed previously you are a character in your life story. Think about what, as a reader, you like to discover about characters when you read. Now think about your own story – will your readers be able to discover those things about you? Although theoretically you should know yourself very well, have you ever listed your attributes on paper? If not, it's time you did.

Take a piece of paper and answer the following questions about yourself:

Age	Person(s) you admire most
Eye colour	Person(s) you admire least
Weight	Favourite relaxation
Height	Favourite place
Marital status	Greatest achievement
Number of children (if any)	5 things I'm proud of
Occupation	5 things I'm not proud of
Favourite colour/food/movie etc	My Hero(es)
Hobbies	Earliest memory
Left or right handed	Favourite quote
Personality type	Places you've travelled to
Greatest fear	Most annoying habit

Consider your story as it is now and ask yourself if you have put across any of these things in your writing. Would a stranger who has read your book be able to answer some basic questions about you and the person you are?

Obviously, you don't want to just list these things. They should be worked into your story at the appropriate time. And in the end you might not be able to get them all in there. But you should try to get as many across to your reader as possible.

Another valuable exercise is to ask these questions about yourself at various points in your life eg at age 15, 25, 35 etc. How have you changed over the years?

FURTHER RESOURCES

There are numerous books out there about writing. Here are a couple to get you started.

Everything I Know About Writing – John Marsden

The Writer's Guide – Irina Dunn

The Elements of Style – William Strunk Jnr and E.B. White (this is an old book but is regarded as many as a bible for the basic rules of writing).

The internet is also a fantastic resource for learning about different aspects of writing. As well as searching for other book titles there are thousands (millions?) of free articles about writing, including exercises that can be used to help novice writers.

WRITING COURSES

Try TAFE (in your particular state) – they have both short courses (on campus) and correspondence (and/or on-line) certificate courses. If you can't find a correspondence course in your state check out other state TAFE directories as they may offer one. Correspondence/on-line courses are generally self-paced, allowing you to study at the rate which suits you and your lifestyle. They also offer support services via phone and internet.

Private colleges such as The Australian College of Journalism (ACJ), Cengage, The Australian Writing Academy and many others offer courses. The internet is the best way to find them. Many universities offer short courses, including Open University and University Of The Third Age. The Writer's Centre in each state also has a lot of information about writing and courses. Beginners courses are the best place to start, but there is nothing to stop you doing another more advanced course after your first if you feel it would be of benefit.

Courses can range widely in price with TAFE generally being the least expensive. Some of the private colleges can be quite pricey, so research well to see what you get for your money. Weigh up if it's better to spend money on editing rather than a course.

ASSISTANCE WITH SELF-PUBLISHING

There are many websites out there that offer help with self-publishing. It can be a bit of a minefield choosing which will give you the best value for your money (and won't rip you off). I have listed two websites below that I have had experience with and who I know look after first-time novice author/self-publishers.

These two websites can help you with every aspect of self-publishing, including e-book conversion and getting your book on all the major bookstore websites.

Finite Publishing: www.finitepublishing.com

Australian E-Book Publisher: www.australianebookpublisher.com.au
Or PH: 0410 381 333

About The Author

I worked for many years as a biographer, helping 'everyday' people compile their life stories. This book was a result of the most practical hints and tips that I shared with people when I worked with them. I am also a writer, having published three novels.

I value all feedback and am happy to answer any questions, so please feel free to contact me via:

Email: info@helenmckenna.com.au
Website: www.helenmckenna.com.au
Facebook: www.facebook.com/HelenMcKenna.Author
Twitter: www.twitter.com/helenmckenna_

www.ingramcontent.com/pod-product-compliance
Lightning Source LLC
Chambersburg PA
CBHW022121280326
41933CB00007B/485